Pink Tax and the Law

The emergence of the terms 'pink tax' and 'tampon tax' in everyday language suggests that women, who already suffer from an economic disadvantage due to the gender wage gap, are put in an even more detrimental position by means of 'discriminatory consumption taxes'. This book is the first conducting a legal analysis to establish to what extent this public perception is accurate.

Does the practice of 'pink tax' effectively amount to a tax in the legal sense? Does the so-called 'tampon tax' genuinely constitute an anomaly within the general consumption tax system? Most importantly, can these two 'taxes' be legally qualified as discriminatory?

This book provides scientific answers to these questions. It first cuts through the existent information clutter by elucidating the pertinent economic, sociological and psychological components of the practices referred to as 'pink tax' and 'tampon tax'. It then proceeds with a thorough legal analysis of all relevant aspects to determine whether women are indeed subject to discriminatory consumption taxes.

It is well-established that women earn less than men. This book investigates if they simultaneously pay more due to 'discriminatory consumption taxes'.

Dr. Alara Efsun Yazıcıoğlu is an assistant professor and an attorney at law. She is specialized in tax law and sports law. She worked formerly as a senior attorney at PwC Turkey, as a legal advisor at Oberson Avocats (Switzerland) and as a teaching and research assistant in tax law at the University of Geneva (Switzerland). She has publications on various aspects of tax law and sports law, including a co-authored practical cases book (*Droit fiscal suisse et international: Recueil de cas pratiques*) published by Helbing Lichtenhahn Verlag.

Pink Tax and the Law

Discriminating Against Women Consumers

Alara Efsun Yazıcıoğlu

Routledge
Taylor & Francis Group
LONDON AND NEW YORK

First published 2018
by Routledge

2 Park Square, Milton Park, Abingdon, Oxfordshire OX14 4RN
52 Vanderbilt Avenue, New York, NY 10017

Routledge is an imprint of the Taylor & Francis Group, an informa business

First issued in paperback 2020

British Library Cataloguing-in-Publication Data
Names: Yazıcıoğlu, Alara Efsun, author.
Title: Pink tax and the law : discriminating against women consumers / Alara Efsun
   Yazıcıoğlu.
Description: Abingdon, Oxon [UK] ; New York, NY : Routledge, 2018. | Includes index.
Identifiers: LCCN 2018014365 | ISBN 9781138597297 (hardback)
Subjects: LCSH: Sex discrimination against women—Law and legislation. | Wages—Sex
   differences. | Taxation of articles of consumption—Law and legislation. | Sales tax—Law
   and legislation. | Women consumers—Legal status, laws, etc. | Consumer protection—Law
   and legislation. | Women's rights. | Feminine hygiene products.
Classification: LCC K3243 .Y39 2018 | DDC 343.05/5082—dc23
LC record available at https://lccn.loc.gov/2018014365

Library of Congress Cataloging-in-Publication Data
A catalog record for this book has been requested

ISBN: 978-1-138-59729-7 (hbk)
ISBN: 978-0-367-60695-4 (pbk)

Typeset in Times
by Apex CoVantage, LLC

To my mother, Gülbin Yazıcıoğlu
And for women

Contents

Acronyms   viii
Acknowledgements   ix

1   Introduction   1

2   Gender versus sex   3

3   Understanding the term 'pink tax'   7

4   The 'pink tax' phenomenon   15

5   The pink tax: the Schrödinger's cat of tax law   40

6   Legal analysis of the 'tampon tax'   58

7   Government intervention   75

8   Conclusion   89

Index   90

Acronyms

CEDAW	The Convention on the Elimination of All Forms of Discrimination Against Women
Directive 2006/112	Council Directive 2006/112/EC of 28 November 2006 on the common system of value added tax, OJ L 347 of 11 December 2006
EU	European Union
GST	Goods and services tax
OECD	Organisation for Economic Co-operation and Development
UK	The United Kingdom
UN	United Nations
US	United States of America
VAT	Value-added tax
WSSCC	Water Supply & Sanitation Collaborative Council

Acknowledgements

I would like to express my deepest gratitude to:

- Hazal Işınsu Türker for her assistance during the initial research process.
- Brianna Ascher, Siobhán Poole and Nicola Sharpe for their precious support in the preparation of this manuscript.
- My parents, Gülbin and Yusuf Yazıcıoğlu, for their constant encouragement and moral support.

"Humankind is composed of two sexes, called woman and man. Is it conceivable for this group to be improved as a whole by the mere improvement of one part, while the other part is neglected? Is it possible for the half of a mass to soar into the skies as long as its other half is chained to the ground?"

Mustafa Kemal Atatürk

1   Introduction

Women earn less than men, and not only due to lack of proper education, heavy burden of unpaid housework they mostly carry alone, low-skilled (and thereby low-wage) jobs that are made predominantly available to them or gender stereotypes constantly undermining their qualities while inflating their 'flaws'. Women earn less even when they overcome all the social, economic and psychological disadvantages, work in high-skilled jobs and provide services, the quality of which is considered to be 'equal' to the ones provided by men. This phenomenon is referred to as the 'gender wage gap'. As established by the indicators prepared by the OECD,[1] the gender wage gap exists in almost every country, may it be as consequential as 36.7%[2] or as 'minor'[3] as 1.8%.[4] In January 2018, Iceland has become the first country in the world to enact a specific law aiming to counteract the gender wage gap. The practice is expected to be entirely eradicated in the country by 2022. Other countries do not seem to follow its example, at least for the moment.[5]

The emergence of the terms 'pink tax' and 'tampon tax' in everyday language suggests that women may also be paying more than men. The terms refer to the additional amounts paid by women to purchase goods and services that are substantially similar to the ones acquired by men at lower prices and to the consumption tax collected on women's sanitary protection products, which are deemed to be 'luxury items'.

To examine whether the public perception is accurate, this book begins by elucidating the proper terminology that needs to be used in the analysis of

---

1 OECD (2018), Gender wage gap (indicator), available online on the following link: https://data.oecd.org/earnwage/gender-wage-gap.htm [last accessed on 16 January 2018].
2 Korea.
3 The term 'minor' is exclusively used to demonstrate the contrast between the two countries. It is by no means intended to underestimate the wage gap.
4 Costa Rica.
5 March 2018.

the two 'taxes'. First, a demarcation of the terms 'gender' and 'sex', which are commonly, yet inaccurately, used as equivalents, is made. The distinction is important, especially in the area of discrimination (Chapter II). Second, the different terms used in everyday language to designate the 'taxes' concerned are examined one by one. It is established that a variety of terms are used interchangeably in relation to two different practices which cannot possibly be designated by the same name and/or regrouped under an umbrella term. The terms 'pink tax' and 'tampon tax' are deemed to be more appropriate than the other terms used, i.e. 'women tax' and 'gender tax'. It is stated that 'pink tax' should be exclusively used to refer to the additional amounts collected from women consumers during the purchase of a wide range of products and services available on the market and 'tampon tax' should be adopted as the proper term designating the consumption tax levied on women's sanitary protection products (Chapter III).

The second stage consists of examining the two concepts separately. First, the rationale behind 'pink tax' is established by means of the underlying social, economic and psychological factors (Chapter IV). Once the intrinsic characteristics of the concept are determined with certainty, a tax law analysis is conducted to figure out whether the so-called 'pink tax' can legally be qualified as a 'tax'. It is concluded that 'pink tax' is not a tax in the legal sense but produces the same economic effect as a fully hidden selective consumption tax (Chapter V). Second, 'tampon tax', which clearly is a consumption tax, is examined in the light of the main specificities of consumption taxes. It is demonstrated that the public reaction against the tax concerned is justified (Chapter VI).

The last part of the analysis concentrates on government intervention. Such an intervention is revealed to be necessary, since the practices concerned are untenable, they constitute 'bad taxes' and, most importantly, they amount to unlawful sex discrimination. A pink tax, expressly targeting women on the sole basis of their sex, amounts to direct sex discrimination. A tampon tax, submitting one sex (female) at a higher rate on purpose, constitutes an implicit bias inherent to the organizational structure of the tax. Both practices violate the principle of non-discrimination protected by constitutional norms and/or provisions of international treaties. Non-discrimination is also considered to constitute one of the general principles of law (Chapter VII).

This book concludes with the examination of the possible means of government intervention. It is argued that the pink tax can effectively be eliminated by adoption of a 'Sex-Based Pricing Repeal Act', and the tampon tax can be either alleviated or eliminated simply by reducing the consumption tax rate applied to women's sanitary protection products. Depending on the concrete circumstances in a given country, it may also be advisable to keep the tampon tax and use the funds collected to support women in need (Chapter VII).

2   Gender versus sex

A Need for distinction

The terms 'gender' and 'sex' tend to be used as equivalents. To many, 'male' and 'masculine' are interchangeable words, just like 'female' and 'feminine' are. This mostly holds true in the area of law as well. Attorneys, courts, and legislators as well as academic writers do not always proceed to a precise demarcation of these two terms.

This tendency may be due to several reasons. First, it may reveal to be more challenging to pinpoint whether a certain legal issue relates to sex, gender or both. Second, not all countries distinguish between the two notions in their own languages; accordingly, 'sex' and 'gender' may simply be covered by a single term.[1] Last but not least, the term 'gender' may be considered as 'more convenient'. For instance, Ruth Bader Ginsburg, one of the first litigators of US Supreme Court sex discrimination cases in the 1970s, stated that "[f]or impressionable minds the word 'sex' may conjure up improper images".[2] Ginsburg thereby found it more fitting to use the term 'gender', which "[would] ward off distracting associations" while remaining grammatically correct.[3]

Regardless of the underlying reasons, it is clear that such a use is far from being accurate. 'Gender' and 'sex' are entirely different concepts, and not distinguishing between them creates an "unfortunate terminological gap".[4] Such a 'gap' is highly likely to undermine the comprehension of the reasoning followed by academic authors and courts as well as the grasp of the exact scope of the laws and regulations enacted by legislators. In other words, the gap provokes confusion. This holds especially true in

1 Gerards, p. 101.
2 Ruth Bader Ginsburg, cited by Case, p. 10.
3 Ernie Freda, cited by Case, p. 10.
4 Case, p. 10.

the area of discrimination. For this reason, the terms 'sex' and 'gender' will be carefully distinguished and be given their genuine meaning throughout this book.

B Definitions of gender and sex

The terms gender and sex are used in a number of domestic acts and statutes, most commonly in birth, death and marriages registration acts and gender recognition acts as well as non-discrimination provisions present in a variety of other acts and statutes, including constitutions. Nonetheless, these terms are not expressly defined in the acts and statutes incorporating them.[5] Indirect definitions may, however, be given. For instance, article 32A of the Australian Births, Deaths and Marriages Registration Act[6] defines sex affirmation procedure as "a surgical procedure involving the alteration of a person's reproductive organs". It derives from this definition that 'sex' is to be determined only in accordance with a person's reproductive organs.

The lack of a definition given by the law compels the courts to provide for the definitions of these two terms in order to distinguish between them in cases where the delineation is essential to the case at hand. Such a necessity occurred, for instance, in *Dobre v National RR Passenger Corp. (Amtrak)*.[7] The competent court defined the concepts concerned as follows: "The term 'sex' [. . .] refers to an individual's distinguishing biological or anatomical characteristics, whereas the term 'gender' refers to an individual's sexual identity".[8]

The elucidation made by the Court is compliant – to a great extent – with the meanings attributed to the terms by other social sciences. Although 'sex' and 'gender' definitions adopted by different social sciences vary to a certain degree,[9] all social sciences seem to agree on the basics. In a nutshell, sex refers to biological differences. Gender, on the other hand, refers to the

5 As per the research conducted by the author.
6 Births, Deaths and Marriages Registration Act 1995 No 62.
7 *Dobre v National RR Passenger Corp. (Amtrak)*, 850 F. Supp. 284 – Dist. Court, ED Pennsylvania 1993.
8 *Ibid*, p. 286.
9 While anthropology offers very clear definitions of the terms 'gender' and 'sex', psychology provides a range of different definitions which are more difficult to delineate (on this point see, for example, Berg, p. 144, Howell and Williams Paris, pp. 87–107 and Muehlenhard and Peterson, pp. 791–803). Sociology, on the other hand, mainly focuses on the cultural and social aspects and on the demarcation of gender differences that are due to cultural/ social environment and the ones that are caused by 'natural' (i.e. biological) elements (the so-called 'nature versus nurture debate') (see, for example, Stockard, pp. 215–217 and Hunter College Women's Studies Collective, pp. 127–137).

cultural and social elements that are expected to be fulfilled by the members of a certain sex.[10]

Sex consists of the 'biological labels' put on human beings at the time of their birth on the basis of a number of anatomical criteria.[11] There are only two such biological labels: female and male.[12] This bipolar construct is universally acknowledged and does not diverge from country to country.[13] The notion of 'gender' is built upon this bipolar construct: two different sexes give rise to two different genders: masculine and feminine. What is being understood by 'masculine' and 'feminine' derives from culture and social influences.[14] Consequently, the behaviours and traits assigned to women and men may vary, at least to a certain extent, from country to country.[15]

As per the social constructionist view, gender is not an attribute of the person (i.e. it is not linked to biological factors) but a performance.[16] In other words, gender is not something we *are* but something we *do*.[17] *Doing gender* requires the fulfilment of both signifying elements and performance elements. A person assumes the signifying elements, such as clothing and hair style, and exhibits the performance elements, such as ways of talking and walking.[18] While sex is something that a person *has* without making an effort, gender needs to be signalled and performed.[19]

It is traditionally assumed that females should demonstrate feminine characteristics and males should exhibit masculine characteristics. The majority of individuals opt for satisfying this social expectation related to their

---

10 'Sexual identity' should be differentiated from 'gender'. 'Sexual identity' can be defined as "one's self-conception as heterosexual, gay or lesbian, bisexual, or transgendered" (Kramer, p. 61). This aspect falls, however, out of the scope of this book and will not be further examined. For more information on this point, see, for example, Kramer, p. 61.

11 Hunter College Women's Studies Collective, p. 127.

12 It is clear that not all human beings can be qualified with certainty as female or male at the moment of their birth. This aspect is, however, not relevant for the purposes of this book.

13 In some countries (namely Australia, Germany, India, Nepal and New Zealand) the official documents mention a 'third sex' (www.thetimes.co.uk/article/germany-to-offer-third-gender-option-on-birth-registers-2sm5w7509 [last accessed on 11 January 2018]; for a legal discussion relating to the 'third sex', see for example, *NSW Registrar of Births, Deaths and Marriages v Norrie* [2014] HCA 11). This 'third sex' encompasses 'intersex' persons. Intersexism is often referred to as a 'rare condition' in the literature. This aspect will not be further developed in this book, since it is not relevant for the purposes of the discussion.

14 Hunter College Women's Studies Collective, p. 139 and Stockard, p. 216–217.

15 Hunter College Women's Studies Collective, p. 127; Giele, p. 294 and Stockard, p. 216.

16 Batalha and Reynolds, p. 173.

17 West Candace and Zimmerman Don H. cited by numerous authors such as Hunter College Women's Studies Collective, p. 137 and Batalha and Reynolds, p. 173.

18 Segal, p. 5.

19 *Ibid.*

'proper gender'. Needless to state, there are exceptions. Individuals from both sexes may choose to perform the gender that is customarily assigned to the other sex or may opt for combining the traits of both genders (the so-called 'androgyny'). Thus, there exist six possible combinations of sex and gender: masculine female, masculine male, feminine female, feminine male, androgynous female and androgynous male.

Bibliography

Batalha Luisa and Reynolds Katherine J., Gender and Personality: Beyond Gender Stereotypes to Social Identity and the Dynamics of Social Change, in Ryan Michelle K. and Branscombe Nyla R. (eds), *The SAGE Handbook of Gender and Psychology*, Sage Publications, 2013.

Berg Gregory E., Sex Estimation of Unknown Human Remains, in Langley Natalie R. and Tersigni-Tarrant MariaTeresa A. (eds), *Forensic Anthropology: A Comprehensive Introduction*, 2nd edition, CRC Press, 2017.

Case Mary Anne, Disaggregating Gender from Sex and Sexual Orientation: The Effeminate Man in the Law and Feminist Jurisprudence, *Yale Law Journal*, Volume 1, Issue 105, 1995–1996, pp. 1–105.

Freda Ernie, Washington in Brief: Clinton's Old Underwear Full of Tax Holes in *Atlanta J. & Constitution*, 1993.

Gerards Janneke, Discrimination Grounds, in Schiek Dagmar, Waddington Lisa and Bell Mark (eds), *Cases, Materials and Text on National, Supranational and International Non-Discrimination Law*, Ius Commune Casebooks for the Common Law of Europe, Hart Publishing, 2007.

Giele Janet Z., Gender and Sex Roles, in Smelser Neil J. (ed), *Handbook of Sociology*, Sage Publications, 1988.

Ginsburg Bader Ruth, Gender in the Supreme Court: The 1973 and 1974 Terms, *Supreme Court Review*, Issue 1, 1975.

Howell Brian M. and Williams Paris Jenell, *Introducing Cultural Anthropology: A Christian Perspective*, Baker Academic, 2011.

Hunter College Women's Studies Collective, *Women's Realities, Women's Choices*, Oxford University Press, 1995.

Kramer Laura, *The Sociology of Gender, A Brief Introduction*, 2nd edition, Roxbury Publishing Company, 2005.

Muehlenhard Charlene L. and Peterson Zoe D., Distinguishing Between Sex and Gender: History, Current Conceptualizations, and Implications, *Sex Roles*, Volume 64, 2011, pp. 791–803.

Segal Edwin S., Cultural Constructions of Gender, in Ember Carol R. and Ember Melvin (eds), *Encyclopedia of Sex and Gender, Men and Women in the World's Cultures*, Volume 1, Kluwer Academic and Plenum Publishers, 2004.

Stockard Jean, Gender Socialization, in Chafetz Saltzman Janet (ed), *Handbook of the Sociology of Gender*, Kluwer Academic and Plenum Publishers, 1999.

West Candace and Zimmerman Don H., Doing Gender, *Gender and Society Journal*, Volume 1, Issue 2, 1987, pp. 125–151.

3 Understanding the term 'pink tax'

'Pink tax' is a recently emerged term that is widely used in everyday life, notably in social media, newspapers and YouTube videos. This chapter aims to clarify the scope of this popular term. To this end, first the colour pink is briefly examined (A). Then, the contours of the concept 'pink tax' are drawn (B).

A 'Pink', an undisputed symbol of femininity

The colour pink is a strong universal symbol of femininity. The identification of women by means of the colour pink may be observed in various areas of everyday life. For instance, items and clothes manufactured for baby girls are predominantly pink; the signature colour of Barbie[1] (claimed to be the favourite doll of little girls) is a specific shade of pink,[2] the rights of which is owned by Mattel;[3] most products destined to be used by women are either manufactured in pink and/or sold in pink packages; the fields of occupation traditionally dominated by women are commonly referred to as 'pink-collar jobs';[4] the 'pink ribbon' is the international symbol for breast

---

1 Produced by Mattel Inc., an American multinational toy manufacturing company.
2 More precisely PMS 219C. Mattel even designed a special Barbie doll with Pantone (an American corporation best known for its Pantone Matching System [PMS], a proprietary colour space used in a variety of industries) for adult collectors. The doll wears a PMS 219C coloured dress made from Pantone colour chips. See Mattel's website for more details on the 'Pink in PANTONE® Barbie® Doll' (http://barbie.mattel.com/shop/en-us/ba/gold-label/pink-in-pantone-barbie-doll-w3376 [last accessed on 14 January 2018]).
3 *Forbes*, In Depth: Barbie By The Numbers, available on the following link: www.forbes.com/2009/03/05/barbie-design-manufacturing-business_numbers_slide/#2beab16614a1 [last accessed on 14 January 2018].
4 The author Louise Kapp Howe played a major role in the definition of the term 'pink-collar' by means of her book titled *Pink Collar Workers*, published in 1977.

cancer awareness; 'pink taxis' destined to provide a safer environment for women are available in a number of countries[5] and extra-large 'pink parking spaces' are at the disposal of female drivers in China.[6]

The emergence of pink as a 'gendered colour' seems to have mainly occurred by means of baby clothing and nursery items. In the 1890s pink and blue were gender-neutral colours, used interchangeably in baby items.[7] In fact, it was even considered that should a preference be made, blue, a more delicate and dainty colour, was more appropriate for girls.[8]

In a rather short period of time, with the undeniable assistance of cloth manufacturers, pink and blue have evolved into 'gendered colours'. To shape customers' choices into a more profitable and predictable pattern and to prevent the handing down of baby clothes from one child to the next (which was effortlessly feasible with gender-neutral colours) as much as possible, cloth manufacturers adopted and applied 'the pink and blue coding'. This clearly discernible colour coding constituted an ideal solution for the industry and was, progressively, adopted by the societies.[9] By the end of the 19th century, it was commonly accepted that "pink was for girls and blue was for boys".[10]

Gradually, the colour pink has become firmly associated with femininity. This association was further strengthened by the clear rejection of the colour pink by feminist parents during the 1960s. As a matter of fact, the straightforward veto of the parents demonstrated the extent to which pink as a gendered colour became embedded in the culture of most countries. The popularity of pink as a 'girl's colour' peaked after 2000.[11]

Peculiarly, despite the fact that pink and blue are often used as counterparts, blue does clearly not wield as strong a symbolic value as pink.[12] It is common for women to use the colour blue on their clothing or other personal items, but it is still extremely rare for men to use pink products. So far, pink has "trumped any and all attempts to neuter it" and remained as the most, and maybe the only, solidly gendered colour.[13]

---

5 India, Egypt and Australia are some of the countries where pink taxis are available.
6 'Pink taxis' and 'pink parking spaces' are measures that are subject to dispute on discrimination grounds. This aspect does not fall within the scope of this book and will not be further developed.
7 Paoletti, pp. 111–114.
8 *Ibid*, p. 109.
9 *Ibid*, p. 117.
10 Mollard-Desfour, p. 31.
11 Paoletti, p. 120.
12 *Ibid*, p. 123.
13 In the 1930s, 'pink' also became the colour of 'homophobia'. This association started in the Nazi concentration camps. Detainees were regrouped in different 'types', and

Even if women's and little girls' preference for the colour pink has been created and strengthened by the baby-product industry and the deeply rooted cultural norms, a common conviction on the 'innate' nature of such a preference exists. The scientific proof of such conviction is still lacking. This being stated, when researched online, a study conducted by neuroscientists Anya C. Hurlbert and Yazhu Ling is often referred to as the scientific basis of women's and little girls' innate preference for pink.[14]

In the study they conducted with 208 subjects, Hurlbert and Ling made important observations on colour preference. Their findings can be summarized, in simple terms, as follows: (i) colour preference of females is more pronounced and sustained compared to males; (ii) both males and females share a natural preference for 'bluish' contrasts (it must be noted that British women weighted bluish contracts significantly higher than their male counterparts); (iii) the average female preference peaks in the 'reddish-purple' region and falls rapidly in the 'greenish-yellow' region and (iv) the male preference is shifted through blue-green.[15] Hurlbert and Ling indicate that the female preference of reddish contrasts and more pronounced colour sensibility of females may be due to the evolutionary division of labour.[16] As gatherers, females had to differentiate edible red leaves embedded in the green foliage.[17]

Although the study conducted by Hurlbert and Ling demonstrates a clear preference of females for 'reddish-purple'[18] contrasts, the underlying

---

each 'type' had to wear a specific coloured symbol (most commonly triangles and stars). The colour assigned to homosexuals was pink. The association between pink and homosexuals was reinforced in the 1980s, when the French press referred to the pandemic of AIDS as '*la peste rose*' (a number of different countries adopted this terminology and used the term 'pink plague' while referring to AIDS). Later on, some homosexual associations began to use the colour pink as their signature colour. Today, pink and homosexuals continue to be linked. This 'link' is, however, much weaker than the link between pink and women (Mollard-Desfour, pp. 32–33 and Agar, p. 59).

14 See, for example, in *Time* magazine, Coco Masters' "Study: Why Girls Like Pink", available on the following link: http://content.time.com/time/health/article/0,8599,1654371,00.html [last accessed on 4 February 2018]; in *The Telegraph*, Roger Highfield's "Girls Really Do Prefer Pink, Study Shows", available on the following link: www.telegraph.co.uk/news/science/science-news/3304225/Girls-really-do-prefer-pink-study-shows.html [last accessed on 4 February 2018] and in the *New Scientist*, Roxanne Khamsi's "Women May Be Hardwired to Prefer Pink", available on the following link: www.newscientist.com/article/dn12512-women-may-be-hardwired-to-prefer-pink/ [last accessed on 4 February 2018].

15 Hurlbert and Ling, p. R624.

16 *Ibid*, p. R625.

17 *Ibid*.

18 Reddish-purple is actually different than pink. Pink is formed by the combination of red and white. Purple, on the other hand, is formed by the combination of red and blue.

reasons of this preference have not been identified by the authors. Hurlbert and Ling indicate that "while these [colour preference] differences may be innate, they may also be modulated by the cultural context or individual experience".[19] On this point, the authors observe that the Chinese subjects gave stronger weighting to reddish colours than the British subjects, which may be due to the Chinese culture, which designates red as the colour of 'good luck'.[20] Thereupon, the study conducted by Hurlbert and Ling, the purpose of which was to demonstrate the predictability of colour preference and not to identify the underlying reasons for such preference, is far from proving that women are disposed to an innate preference for pink, as is indicated in numerous non-scientific newspaper and magazine articles.

Women's preference for pink seems to be embedded in cultural norms that were cultivated by regular efforts of their societies. Whether due to cultural norms or biological facts, it is undisputed that pink is a strong symbol of femininity. Accordingly, it is possible to deduce that the so-called 'pink tax' is a tax intended to be imposed on women.

B Concept of the 'pink tax'

B.1   Use of the term 'pink tax' in everyday language

Although it is not possible to trace back the origins of the term 'pink tax' with certainty, the concept seems to have emerged as a result of the campaign conducted by Georgette Sand, a French women's rights group. Georgette Sand initiated an online petition on *change.org* titled '*Monoprix: Stop aux produits plus chers pour les femmes! #Womantax*'[21] in October 2014. In a couple of months, the term 'woman tax' evolved into '*taxe rose*', the French term for 'pink tax'.[22] It is not possible to pinpoint the underlying reasons of this evolution. However, it can be safely assumed that the shift is due to the colour of the products that were over-priced. The flagship products

---

Accordingly, the results of the study concerned seem to be demonstrating women's preference for the colours red, blue and the combination of these two colours (for more information on the formation of colours, see, for example, Mollard-Desfour, pp. 16–18).

19 Hurlbert and Ling, p. R625.

20 *Ibid.*

21 The title of the petition can be translated as '*Monoprix: Stop more expensive products for women # Womantax*' (translated by the author). Monoprix is a French retail chain selling a great variety of products including food, hardware and clothing. The online petition, which has ended, can be consulted on the following link: www.change.org/p/monoprix-stop-aux-produits-plus-chers-pour-les-femmes-womantax [last accessed on 5 February 2017].

22 On this point, see the website of Georgette Sand: www.georgettesand.org/categorie-on-agit/taxe-rose/ [last accessed on 5 February 2017].

chosen to raise awareness to the cause were pink razors and their blue counterparts. The use of the traditional pink and blue coding most likely served to the vulgarization of the argument that was being made, aiming to ensure thereby a greater public reaction. The emphasis on the colour pink may also be observed in the *tweet* posted by Pascale Boistard, the French state secretary for women's rights, on 31 October 2014 to increase public alertness on the issue: *"Le rose est-il une couleur de luxe? #womantax"*.[23]

The debate initiated in France echoed in a great number of other countries in a time span as short as a year. The discussion became much more broadly mediatized following a study conducted by the New York City Department of Consumer Affairs in December 2015. The study, titled *'From Cradle to Cane: The Cost of Being a Female Consumer'*, demonstrated that on average women's products cost 7% more than similar products for men.[24] Although the study did not proceed with an estimation of the annual financial impact of the pink tax, the findings suggested that "women [were] paying thousands of dollars more over the course of their lives to purchase similar products as men".[25]

Following the publication of the study, 'pink tax' became an extremely popular topic, forming the subject matter of many newspaper and magazine articles,[26] TV programs and YouTube videos. The terms 'pink tax', 'woman tax' (or 'women tax') and 'gender tax' begun to be used as synonyms in these publications and videos as well as in social media platforms.

The debate swiftly spread to another tax: the so-called 'tampon tax'. The term 'tampon tax' refers to the consumption tax collected upon tampons and sanitary pads. The increased awareness of the 'pink tax' resulted in the 'tampon tax' being perceived as another layer of 'pink tax' (or 'woman tax' or 'gender tax'). Even though 'tampon tax' is generally differentiated from 'pink tax', the instances in which they are used as equivalents are more than rare. For example, Boxed Wholesale, an online retailer, has created a specific category of products titled '#Rethink Pink'.[27] The retailer's website clearly indicates (in pink) that 'no pink tax' is levied upon the women's products falling within that category. The products concerned include not

23 The tweet can be translated as *"I Is pink a luxury colour? #womantax"* (translated by the author).
24 From Cradle to Cane, p. 5.
25 *Ibid*, p. 6.
26 See, for example, in *Forbes*, Ian Ayres' "Which Retailers Charge the Largest 'Pink Tax'", available on the following link: www.forbes.com/sites/whynot/2016/01/07/which-retailers-charge-the-largest-pink-tax/#34ada8585462 [last accessed on 5 February 2018].
27 #RethinkPink, www.boxed.com/products/highlight/164/rethinkpink/ [last accessed on 4 February 2018].

only shampoos, shower gels and deodorants (typical examples of products that suffer from over-pricing) but also tampons and sanitary pads.

It is possible to conclude that a number of different terms are currently being used as equivalents to describe two distinct types of tax. This confusion reigning in everyday language must be elucidated before further examination of these taxes.

B.2   From confusion to clarity: a specific term for each different concept

To proceed to a legal analysis of 'pink tax', it is first necessary to examine the variety of terms used to designate the same or similar concept(s) and to determine which of these terms are the most appropriate. As described in the previous subsection, 'pink tax' seems to be used interchangeably with the terms 'gender tax'[28] and 'woman tax'[29] (or 'women tax') to designate the additional amount charged on pink products. 'Pink tax' is also occasionally used to designate the so-called 'tampon tax' (i.e. the additional amount charged on women sanitary protection products), although it is not considered as being an exact equivalent of this latter term.

It is clear that the burden of both 'taxes'[30] lies upon women consumers. This does not entail, however, that the taxes concerned are similar from a legal standpoint. In fact, as will be demonstrated in this book, these two types of 'additional amounts' differ from each other in a significant manner from a tax law perspective. They constitute, thereby, completely distinct concepts that can neither be designated by the same term nor be regrouped under the same category. Consequently, two separate terms need to be determined to refer to these two dissimilar taxes.

Taxes are traditionally named after their object (i.e. the sum/item/transaction/situation in respect of which the tax is levied) and not their subject (i.e. persons liable to pay the tax concerned, typically referred to as 'taxpayers'). For instance, the tax collected on income is named 'income tax' and not 'income earner tax', the tax levied on inheritance is labelled as 'inheritance tax' and not as 'inheritor tax' and the tax collected from a

---

28 Most commonly in the US.
29 Most commonly used in France.
30 In this subsection, the reference is made to 'taxes', since these concepts are commonly being referred to as 'taxes'. Whether they effectively constitute a tax is analyzed in the following chapters. The author does not intend to imply that both concepts can legally be qualified as a 'tax'.

number of products containing sugar is referred to as 'sugar tax' and not as 'consumer of sugary products tax'.

Subsequently, the terms 'gender tax' and 'woman tax' are not suitable to designate either of the taxes under examination. The term 'gender tax' fails to elucidate not only the object (i.e. the products that are being taxed) but also the subject (i.e. women consumers) of the taxes concerned. As explained in Chapter II, 'gender' is far from being the equivalent of 'women'. It can, therefore, safely be stated that 'gender tax' constitutes a blurry term that is best avoided. The term 'woman tax', on the other hand, is indicative of the taxpayers of both taxes. It is, thereby, somewhat more convenient than 'gender tax'. Nonetheless, since taxes are customarily named in accordance with their object, the term 'woman tax' is highly likely to give rise to the false premise that 'woman' constitutes the object of the tax. In other words, it incorrectly implies that the tax becomes due by the sheer fact of being a woman rather than by the purchase of certain products. Thus, the term 'woman tax' is not adequate to designate the taxes under examination either.

The terms that can be retained are, therefore, pink tax and tampon tax. They specifically refer to the objects (respectively pink products and sanitary protection products) of the taxes concerned. The first category, i.e. the additional amount charged on 'pink products', should be designated as the 'pink tax'. The second category, i.e. the additional amount charged on women's sanitary protection products, should be designated as the 'tampon tax'.

For the sake of clarity, throughout this book, the reference will only be made to the terms 'pink tax' and 'tampon tax' as defined in this subsection, except in cases where other terms were used by the competent authorities enacting official documents, such as laws, regulations and reports. In such cases, the proposed term instead of the term that has been used by the competent authority will be signalled in the corresponding footnote.

Bibliography

Books and academic articles

Agar James N., Queer in France: AIDS Dissidentification in France, in Downing Lisa and Gillett Robert (eds), *Queer in Europe, Contemporary Case Studies*, Routledge, 2011.
Hurlbert Anya C. and Ling Yazhu, Biological Components of Sex Differences in Color Preference, *Current Biology*, Volume 17, Issue 16, 2007, pp. R623–R625.
Mollard-Desfour Annie, *Le Dictionnaire des Mots et Expressions de Couleur du XXᵉ Siècle, Le Rose*, CNRS Editions, 2002.
Paoletti Jo B., *Pink and Blue, Telling the Boys from the Girls in America*, Indiana University Press, 2012.

Studies

From Cradle to Cane: The Cost of Being a Female Consumer, New York City Department of Consumer Affairs, December 2015, available on the following link: https://www1.nyc.gov/assets /dca/downloads/pdf/partners/Study-of-Gender-Pricing-in-NYC.pdf [last accessed on 16 February 2018] (cited as From Cradle to Cane).

4 The 'pink tax' phenomenon

The pink tax is a complex phenomenon formed by different, but equally important, layers. It is the end result of the combination of a variety of social, economic and psychological trends. To understand what the pink tax really is, one must understand all the different dynamics involved.

To this end, this chapter begins by making general observations on consumption (A). These general observations form the rationale behind the *'shrink it, pink it and women will buy it to a higher price'* opinion put forward by a number of journalists and politicians (B). When put to a scientific test, however, this opinion is proven to be erroneous (C). As a matter of fact, the pink tax is not a problem caused by women consumers. Quite the opposite: it is the result of a practice called 'gender-based pricing' put in place by producers/providers of goods/services (D). Women consumers are suffering from the consequences of this practice that cannot be avoided, even by the most draconian efforts (E). Whether this practice should be perpetuated or put to an end is a predominantly political question (F).

A General observations on consumption

To understand the pink tax phenomenon, first the following general observations on consumption need to be made:

1 The market constitutes the main channel of consumption.
2 As per the predominant economic theory, consumers are making their decisions in a well-informed, rational and selfish manner. In the same vein, producers act rationally and opt for policies that will allow them to maximize their benefits. The market finds, thus, its perfect equilibrium on its own.
3 The 'hyper-rationality' assumed by the predominant economic theory does not seem to exist in practice. Research shows that consumers tend to demonstrate self-control problems.
4 A product or a service is not purchased merely on its intrinsic qualities anymore; the message it sends is as important as its qualities.

A.1   The market: the main channel of consumption

Goods and services can be provisioned by three different means: (i) through the state (such as health care and waste collection), (ii) through interpersonal networks (for instance, friends and family who provide goods and services via informal help and gifts) and (iii) through markets.[1]

The market is the only channel that enables individuals to acquire the goods and services of their choice whenever they desire and at the location they prefer. The two other channels lack such flexibility in terms of goods and services that may be obtained (which are limited), timing of acquisition (which is usually not determined on the sole basis of consumers' intent) and location of obtainment (which is generally subject to restrictions).

Consequently, to acquire the majority of goods and services, individuals must have recourse to the market. It is, therefore, undisputable that the market constitutes, by far, the most frequently used channel by consumers.

A.2   Predominant view: individuals are free, just as markets should be

The dominant school of economics, the neoclassical school, views individuals as selfish, rational and well-informed beings. Consumers are assumed to make only the consumption choices that will maximize their own, or at most their family members', welfare.[2] Individuals are also considered to make exclusively rational choices, enabling them to achieve a given goal in the most cost-efficient manner.[3] This 'hyper-rationality' entails that consumers are 'market mavens', i.e. they are extremely well-informed on the variety of products and services offered in the market as well as their prices.[4] The human being is thus perceived as a machine devoted to the maximization of pleasure (utility) and the minimization of pain.[5]

As per the dominant approach, each individual has a freely determined list of preferences, i.e. goods and services that he/she likes. By comparing the prices of different services and goods available on the market, the consumer chooses a combination of goods and services that maximize

---

1 Southerton, p. 134.
2 Chang, *Economics*, p. 173.
3 *Ibid.*
4 The term 'maven' can be defined as one who accumulates knowledge. 'Market maven' and 'price vigilante' are terms that are used to designate individuals who are extremely well-informed on products/services available on the market, as well as their prices. For more information on this point, see Gladwell, pp. 60–69.
5 Chang, *Economics*, p. 121.

his/her utility. The individual choices made by consumers form the demand curve, demonstrating to the producers what the demands are for their goods and services at different prices. The quantity of goods and services that the producers are willing to provide at each price (i.e. the supply curve) is determined by the producers' rational choices, made with a view of maximizing their profits. The market reaches its equilibrium where the two curves meet.[6] The rationality of all economic actors as well as the competition among producers allows the market to self-equilibrate. As a general rule, the inner dynamics of the market should not be interfered with, except in cases where the market prices fail to reflect the true social costs and benefits (the so-called 'market failure').[7] Since the 1980s, many neoclassical economists developed theories, such as the 'rational expectation' theory in macroeconomics and the 'efficient market hypothesis' in financial economics, arguing that market failures are not likely to occur in practice and since economic agents are rational, the market is bound to outcome efficient when left alone.[8] Simultaneously, the government failure argument, according to which the market failure itself cannot justify government intervention as governments risk failure even more seriously than the markets do, was also invoked.[9] These theories are still predominant.

To sum up, consumers are free to acquire whatever they desire, as long as they are willing to pay the 'right' price for it, which is determined by producers that 'rationally' fix the price of the goods and services they freely choose to provide. It is argued that the government intervention in this perfectly self-equilibrating system should be kept to a strict minimum.

A.3 Self-control problem: endless appeal of 'in sight, in mind' and 'right here, right now'

One of the flaws of the dominant economic theory is its overestimation of human 'qualities'. No individual can demonstrate the 'Olympian rationality' presumed by the dominant approach. Quite the opposite: research proves that human beings possess only 'bounded rationality'. The available studies on the matter firmly establish that individuals are prone to a long list of biases and fallacies, such as the sunk cost fallacy, the endowment effect and loss aversion.[10] Far from being the 'machine' suggested by the

---

6 *Ibid*, pp. 173–174.
7 *Ibid*, p. 123.
8 *Ibid*, p. 125.
9 *Ibid*.
10 For more information on these biases and fallacies, see, for example, Dobelli, pp. 17–20, 72–75 and 100–103.

predominant view, humans operate with an intuitive and heuristic system of thinking, which often results in poor logical analysis.[11] On top of this 'logical reasoning problem', individuals deal with a more serious issue on a daily basis: self-control.

Thaler uses the example of a bowl of cashews to illustrate both the self-control problem and the decay between the hyper-rational individual suggested by the dominant view ('Econ') and the 'real' individual ('Human'). A hypothetical conversation between a Human removing a tempting bowl of cashews in order to stop eating and an Econ would be as follows:

> ECON: Why did you remove the cashews?
>
> HUMAN: Because I did not want to eat any more of them.
>
> ECON: If you did not want to eat any more nuts, then why go to the trouble of removing them? You could have simply acted on your preferences and stopped eating.
>
> HUMAN: I removed the bowl because if the nuts were still available, I would have eaten more.
>
> ECON: In that case, you prefer to eat more cashews, so removing them was stupid.[12]

There exist several methods suggested by the psychology and the behavioural economics literature to cope with the self-control problem. While the details relating to such methods fall outside the scope of this book, it is important to note the two following points regarding self-control: (i) limiting one's own choices by removing the tempting product is an efficient and frequently used method ('out of sight, out of mind')[13] and (ii) individuals are prone to prefer immediate rewards over future benefits ('right here, right now').[14]

A.4 Consuming symbols

As put forward by Karl Marx, the industrial society altered the meaning of goods. Prior to industrialization, the value of goods was determined in accordance with objective criteria including the amount of labour necessary for their production, the quality of the materials used and the usefulness of the product (the so-called 'use value'). Industrial production made it difficult to have any sense of the labour involved in producing goods. As a result, the use value was gradually replaced with 'the symbolic value'. The

---

11 Chang, *Economics*, p. 199.
12 Thaler, p. 86.
13 *Ibid*, p. 100.
14 *Ibid*, p. 90.

value of a product is no longer determined exclusively by the labour force and the materials used in its production but also by 'its symbolic meaning', such as being a 'designer' or a 'limited edition' item.[15] In other words, the value of a product also depends on how much the product is valued by potential consumers, for one reason or another.[16] The same reasoning may also be extended to services. Prices of services rendered do not merely reflect costs and efforts of service providers, they also reflect the 'prestige' of their establishments.

What is being exchanged is no longer a mere good or service, it is a sign and an image.[17] More plainly put, consumers pay for symbols. The willingness of consumers to pay extra amounts for symbolic significance of goods and services finds its roots in large urban environments, developed mostly as a result of the industrialization process. The faceless and impersonal nature of large urban environments led consumption to become a unique way to express oneself and to reassert a sense of individuality in the anonymity of the everyday life.[18] Consumption, thus, replaced production and became a principle source of human identity. This tendency observed in sociology finds its equivalent in economics: the neoclassical view shifted the focus of economics from production to consumption and exchange.[19] The economic system is currently envisaged as a web of exchanges, ultimately driven by the choices made by 'sovereign' consumers.[20]

It can, therefore, be stated that as rational consumers, individuals choose to purchase symbols for a variety of reasons. They express their belonging to a certain lifestyle, social aspirations and identity by means of the products and services they are purchasing. They relate to one another and understand, interpret and relate to the world they live in through consumption.[21] Quite reasonably, the market responds to this fundamental desire of individuals: it allows them to consume symbols at the prices that they are willing to pay.

B Shrink it, pink it and women will buy it at a higher price

As per an opinion expressed by certain journalists, bloggers, politicians and individuals, the pink tax issue can simply be summarized as '*shrink it, pink it and women will buy it at a higher price*' (hereinafter 'the shrink it-pink

15 Southerton, p. 136.
16 Chang, *Economics*, p. 121.
17 Southerton, p. 136.
18 *Ibid*, pp. 135–136.
19 Chang, *Economics*, p. 121.
20 *Ibid*, p. 122.
21 Southerton, pp. 135–137.

it opinion'). For instance, in his article published in *Forbes*, the author Tim Worstall argues that "Absolutely no legislative relief is necessary here. Everyone's already got the choice and that they make the choices they do shows that they're entirely happy with the choices they are making".[22] Similarly, in her article published on the website of the Independent Women's Forum, Hadley Heath states that

> Men and women are different. Our preferences are different, and our needs are different, too. My husband can get away with a dab of shampoo, sure, but I have longer hair than him and will go through my Herbal Essences bottles faster than he'll get through his Pantene Classic Clean Two-in-One. (Two-in-one? Not for me!) [and that] If you don't like the "pink tax", then you don't have to play the game. Buy the men's products. Or better yet, buy whatever's on clearance.[23]

A comparable approach can also be observed in the recent (2016) legislative debate that took place in California. In an attempt to further engage in the fight against price differences based exclusively on sex, the State of California sought to amend its Gender Tax[24] Repeal Act of 1995.[25] The 2016 amendment, which finally was **not adopted** by the Assembly, would have extended the scope of the Gender Tax Repeal Act, which is currently limited to services, to products. During the hearing that took place on 28 June 2016, a number of arguments were advanced by both the supporters and the opponents of the amendment bill. The following passage taken from the Bill Analysis is in line with the shrink it-pink it opinion:

> Indeed, one might argue that this bill is premised on the sexist belief that women are not as strong as men when it comes to resisting marketing pressures and have no choice but to choose pink razors over blue razors, even if the pink razors are more expensive. Opponents, on the other hand, contend that men and women are equally capable of making informed choices. Parents, for example, can opt for the $25 blue

---

22 In *Forbes*, Tim Worstall, "The Pink Tax Is Nothing to Do with Public Policy, Women Can Solve It for Themselves", available on the following link: www.forbes.com/sites/ timworstall/2014/11/13/the-pink-tax-is-nothing-to-do-with-public-policy-women-can-solve-it-for-themselves/#82399f3677b5 [last accessed on 16 February 2018].

23 *Independent Women's Forum*, Headley Heath, "Ladies, Don't Fall for Pink Tax Myth", available on the following link: http://iwf.org/blog/2799310/Ladies,-Don't-Fall-for-%22Pink-Tax%22-Myth [last accessed on 16 February 2018].

24 'Gender tax' refers to 'pink tax', as per the term adopted in this book.

25 Assembly Bill No. 1088, Civil rights: Gender discrimination, State of California.

scooter over the $50 pink scooter. The parents can teach their daughter an important lesson about gender stereotyping and save $25 to boot.[26]

This approach indicates that women willingly opt for paying the pink tax in order to acquire the products and the 'symbols' of their choice. They make the decision of reimbursing this additional amount to purchase 'pink' (the ultimate symbol of femininity) products and/or to purchase products that are suited to their 'special needs'. Women who complain about paying the pink tax 'without realizing' or 'because they were under the obligation to do so' simply have to find their inner selfish and rational market maven. In other words, they should 'man up', start realizing their self-control problems and become rational consumers like they are supposed to be. If they fail to do so, it is not the problem of the market or the government, it is their personal problem. The government should not interfere with the equilibrium of the market to protect the interests of consumers who cannot control their own will. Producers are certainly not under the obligation to stop selling cashews on the sole basis that some people tend to eat a bowl of them against their best interest. There is no reason to make an exception for the bowl of pink marshmallows.

C The bowl of pink marshmallows

The shrink it-pink it opinion implies that a part of women complaining about the existence of the pink tax are, in fact, suffering from a self-control problem when in the presence of pink products. They cannot resist the temptation of purchasing over-priced pink razors, despite the fact that blue razors are identical to the latter except for their colour.

Women have traditionally been considered as members of the 'weaker sex'. In the study they conducted in 25 countries (including countries from Africa, Asia, Europe, North America, Oceania and South America), Best and Williams found that women were associated with the following adjectives (among others): dependent, meek, dreamy, sentimental, submissive and weak; whereas men were associated with the following adjectives (among others): assertive, confident, dominant, forceful, independent, logical, rational, realistic, serious, strong and wise.[27] Women are perceived to be weaker than men in many tasks, such as financial decision-making, problem-solving, managerial tasks, driving, leadership and political knowledge.[28] Therefore, it is unavoidable for the pink tax debate to concentrate, at least partly, on the will power of women.

---

26 State of California, Bill Analysis, SB 899, p. 12.
27 Best, pp. 13–14.
28 Betz, Ramsey and Sekaquaptewa, p. 432.

Social perceptions, especially those related to differences between men and women, tend to be predominantly cultural. They generally lack any scientific basis and are proven to be erroneous when scientifically researched.[29] The lack of a reliable basis does not, however, prevent social perceptions from forming an information clutter and perpetuating their existence in the minds of the general public.

When it comes to the self-control and will power of individuals, there exists a high-quality weapon that can cut through any information clutter: the 'Marshmallow Test'.

The Marshmallow Test was specifically designed to measure the willpower, i.e. the ability to delay gratification and resist temptations, of individuals.[30] The test created by the psychologist Walter Mischel was first conducted in the 1960s with pre-schoolers at Stanford University's Bing Nursery School.[31] It consisted of a simple challenge: Mischel and his students presented the children with a choice between one reward (for instance, a marshmallow) that they could consume immediately and a larger reward (two marshmallows) for which they would have to wait, alone, for up to 20 minutes. At any moment during the waiting period, the children could stop the experiment by ringing the bell and asking the researcher to hand them the one marshmallow.[32]

Through periodic monitoring of the participant children, Mischel demonstrated that the test results of the pre-schoolers efficiently predicted their future lives. The more seconds the infants were able to delay gratification, the higher their college-admission SAT[33] scores were, the better their rated social and cognitive functioning in their adolescence was, the lower their body mass index was, the better they coped with stress and frustration, the better they pursued their goals and the more developed their sense of self-worth was.[34]

Throughout the countless research and studies he conducted, Mischel observed that even when the reward values were equated and the motivation was the same, girls usually waited **longer** than boys.[35] Mischel indicates that this "greater willingness and the ability of girls to wait longer" is consistent with the finding that throughout the school years, at least in the US, girls are generally rated **higher** on self-discipline measures than boys by

---

29 See, for example, Hunter College Women's Studies Collective, pp. 123 and 128–135.
30 Mischel, pp. 5–6.
31 *Ibid*, p. 4.
32 *Ibid*.
33 Scholastic Aptitude Test, widely used for college admissions in the US.
34 Mischel, p. 5.
35 *Ibid*, p. 47.

their teachers, their parents and themselves.[36] This observation is also sup-ported by other similar studies. For instance, on hypothetical choices about delayed rewards, such as "Would you prefer $55 today or $75 in 61 days?", girls choose the delayed reward more often than boys.[37]

Mischel states that although sex differences on the Marshmallow Test are not always apparent and the research on the matter is ongoing, "on the whole girls seem to have an advantage in the cognitive self-control skills and motivations that enable delay of gratification, at least in the populations and age groups studied so far".[38]

In the light of the research and studies conducted by Mischel, which constitute the most renowned and thorough study available on the matter, women do not seem to systematically fail their 'pink' marshmallow test. On the contrary, their scores are consistently better than men. With this obser-vation, it is apparent that the pink tax problem does not reside in women's self-control mechanism. In other words, the argument according to which a reasonable amount of determination and self-control is sufficient to avoid the pink tax, clearly does not hold water.

Women are not the irrational customers they are assumed to be by the opponents of the pink tax problem. Research clearly shows that they are not that tempted by the sight of a bowl of pink marshmallows and that they are good at delaying rewards. As a matter of fact, men are more tempted by the sight of a bowl of blue marshmallows, and they are not as successful as women in delaying rewards. Yet, a 'blue tax' does not exist, whereas the 'pink tax' constitutes a significant problem.

The predominant economic theory would dictate that this occurrence is certainly the result of a perfectly rational phenomenon: women are ready to pay more for pink products and/or for the products adapted to their needs (which are more sophisticated when compared to men's), whereas men sim-ply do not attach that much importance to the products they purchase, and their needs are considerably less elaborate than women's needs. This argu-ment should be tested in the light of the practice giving rise to the pink tax: gender-based pricing.[39]

---

36 *Ibid*, p. 48.
37 *Ibid*.
38 *Ibid*.
39 It is important to note that the accurate term would be 'sex-based pricing', and not 'gender-based pricing', since the price difference is based on the sex of individuals (i.e. female or male) and not on their gender (i.e. feminine, masculine and androgynous). Nonetheless, the term 'gender-based pricing' will be used throughout this book, since it entered common usage.

D Underlying problem: gender-based pricing

Defining gender-based pricing is an easy task (D.1). Determining its extent is revealed to be effortless too, since a number of studies on the issue were already conducted both by governmental organizations and other researchers (D.1). Examining the 'behind-the-scenes' of gender-based pricing is much more cumbersome and requires a multi-disciplinary approach (D.2).

D.1 Definition and extent

Gender-based pricing can be defined as "the practice of charging different prices for goods or services based on the consumer's gender".[40] As it can be deduced by this definition and demonstrated by the studies reported here, gender-based pricing (and thereby the pink tax) is not exclusively limited to products. Although largely left out from the ongoing public debate on the pink tax, the practice concerned also covers services rendered to women.

Gender-based pricing formed the subject matter of a number of studies conducted both by governmental organizations and academicians in the last two decades. Initially, the research exclusively focused on services. At a later stage, it was extended to products. Regardless of their scope (service, product or both), all studies[41] reached the same result: women are being charged more than men for **substantially similar** products and services.

The main conclusions reached on gender-pricing of **services** can be summarized by means of the following studies and their findings:

•   A survey conducted by the California Assembly Office of Research in 1993 found that women were charged more than men for some services, namely haircut and dry-cleaning.[42] The research established that this 'tax' amounted to approximately $1.351 per woman *per annum*, amounting to $15 million *per annum* for all women in California.[43]

•   In a similar study conducted by the New York City Department of Consumer Affairs in 1992, titled '*Gypped by Gender: A Study of Price Bias against Women in the Marketplace*', it was concluded that women were charged more than men at used car dealers, dry-cleaners, launderers (27% more) and hair salons (23% more).[44]

---

40 Guidance on Gender-Based Pricing, State of Vermont, p. 1.
41 To the extent researched by the author.
42 Harvard Law Review, pp. 1839–1840.
43 *Ibid.*
44 From Cradle to Cane, p. 15.

- In a study they published in 2000, Liston-Heyes and Neokleous[45] demonstrated that women were charged higher prices for haircuts even in cases where they specifically asked for hairstyles identical to men.[46] Liston-Heyes and Neokleous noted that the hair-cutting technology and the training required for a hairdresser to work in a hair salon as well as the wages paid to hairdressers were all identical (substantially similar for wages) for the purposes of haircuts for women and men forming the basis of their study.[47] They also established that even if variables, such as hair length and duration of service, that may influence the pricing of the service did effectively exist, pricing policies were often based not upon such variables but upon sex itself.[48]
- In a study they conducted in 2011, Duesterhaus, Grauerholz, Weichsel and Guittar examined the prices offered by 100 dry-cleaners randomly selected out of 784 listed in the yellow pages. They found that a high pricing disparity existed for shirts. The average dry-clean cost of a men's shirt was $2.06, whereas it was $3.95 for a women's shirt. The disparity existed before additional costs that were incurred due to the fabric of the shirt, its embellishments and/or pleats. In other words, this considerable price gap existed for shirts that were completely identical except for their label: one was labelled as a 'men's shirt' and the other as a 'women's shirt'.[49]
- The State of Vermont's inquiry about dry-cleaning services' price disparities established that women were charged up to $5.20 more than men per shirt. The service providers indicated the prices on the phone, without seeing the specificities of the shirts concerned. When the investigator requested an explanation for the price difference, none of the dry-cleaners could provide any viable justifications.[50]
- A survey examining department stores established that in some stores men usually received complimentary tailoring services, whereas women were charged for the exact same services.[51]

45 Listen-Heyes Catherine and Neokleous Elena, Gender-Based Pricing in the Hairdressing Industry, *Journal of Consumer Policy*, Volume 23, Issue 2, 2000, pp. 107–126.
46 Duesterhaus, Grauerholz, Weichsel and Guittar, p. 178.
47 *Ibid.*
48 *Ibid.*
49 *Ibid*, pp. 181–182.
50 Guidance on Gender-Based Pricing, State of Vermont, p. 7.
51 Harvard Law Review, p. 1840.

The main conclusions reached on gender-pricing of **products** can be described by means of the following studies and their findings:

• The 2015 study of the New York City Department of Consumer Affairs showed that women's products cost 7% more than similar products for men.[52] For the purposes of the study, the Department analyzed more than 90 brands encompassing approximately 800 individual products.[53] The products selected by the Department, varying from toys to adult diapers, were analogous men's and women's products that were closest in branding, ingredients, appearance, textile, construction and/or marketing.[54] The chosen products were strikingly similar, some showing only minor variations from their 'male counterpart' (mostly in their colour and packaging) and some showing no visible differences at all. It was established that such insignificant differences gave rise to a considerable price gap: a red scooter for children cost $24.99, whereas an identical but pink scooter cost $49.99; a men's shirt cost $30, whereas an extremely similar women's shirt of the same brand cost $40; a 3-in-1 men's shampoo cost $1.29, while a 2-in-1 women's shampoo of the same brand cost $1.99.[55]

• In the study they conducted in 2011, Duesterhaus, Grauerholz, Weichsel and Guittar examined a total amount of 538 products, including 199 deodorants, 89 shaving gel/creams, 204 razors and 46 body sprays.[56] They determined that on average: (i) per ounce of deodorant, women paid $1.44, while men paid $1.15; (ii) for a container of body spray women paid $5.81, whereas men paid $4.58; (iii) for one razor, women paid $3.00, while men paid $2.67 and (iv) per ounce of shaving gel, women paid $0.45, while men paid $0.47.[57]

As illustrated by these numerous studies, and many others that were not mentioned here, gender-pricing constitutes a problem that cannot be simply explained by the willingness of women to pay an additional amount for 'feminine' products and/or for products adapted to their 'special needs'. Gender-based pricing consists of charging women more than men on a number of substantially similar products and services and/or providing benefits exclusively to men on certain services for no apparent reason. Branding,

52 From Cradle to Cane, p. 5.
53 *Ibid*, p. 17.
54 *Ibid*.
55 *Ibid*, pp. 7–12.
56 Duesterhaus, Grauerholz, Weichsel and Guittar, pp. 179–180.
57 *Ibid*, p. 183.

ingredients, appearance, textile, construction, efforts put into production, marketing and other potential differences that may exist between women's products and men's products as well as between services rendered to women and services rendered to men were all taken into consideration by a significant number of researchers, who all reached the same conclusion: gender-based pricing can be justified neither by the use value of the products and services concerned nor by their symbolic value (a white women's shirt cannot be considered as having a higher symbolic value than a white men's shirt bearing the same brand; similarly, a dry-cleaning service provided by the same establishment cannot be considered as having a higher symbolic value for women).

The pink tax is not due to women's lack of self-control. It is not due to their willingness to pay an additional amount to acquire certain products or services, either. It is exclusively due to a practice called gender-based pricing. The practice does exist in a number of countries, and it does constitute a problem.

D.2 The making of gender-based pricing

Behind the scenes, gender-based pricing is extremely colourful. It combines a variety of approaches, trends and developments from a number of disciplines. This cultural, sociological, psychological and economic phenomenon is a genuine multi-disciplinary concept. To cover the basics, three main components will be analyzed in detail: gender stereotypes (D.2.1), gendered products (D.2.2) and the importance of physical appearance (D.2.3).

D.2.1 Gender stereotypes: the solid foundation of gender-based pricing

"Individuals are products of their societies."

—Ha-Joon Chang[58]

Gender is a culturally based complex of norms, values and behaviours that a particular society assigns to one biological sex,[59] and that is likely to vary through time in accordance with the historical and economic developments of the society concerned.[60] What is considered appropriate behaviour for

58 Chang, *Economics*, p. 195.
59 Segal, p. 3.
60 Best, p. 21.

women and men varies across societies, but every society, at least to some degree, assigns traits and tasks on the basis of gender.[61] The societal sex/gender schemas traditionally follow a binary system. There are two sexes (female and male), and there exist two genders attributable to these two sexes (feminine and masculine).[62] The commonly presumed sex/gender combinations are 'feminine female' and 'masculine male'. The individual characteristics that are considered to be 'gender-appropriate' include physical, psychological and behavioural traits that may be considered as acceptable for the 'gender labels'. Since there are two different genders, it is commonly assumed that the characteristics borne by one gender are the opposite of (or simply differ from) the characteristics borne by the other.[63]

Societies teach each and every society member the prescribed gender roles by means of a process commonly referred to as 'gender socialization'. Gender socialization of an individual begins with one rather short exclamatory sentence: 'It's a girl!' or 'It's a boy!'.[64] Parents and similar significant others[65] of an infant form the first step of the process. Parents usually demonstrate the following tendencies: (i) choose gender-appropriate toys; (ii) opt for gender-appropriate appearance and clothing (such as putting bows in a girl's hair and dressing their children in 'gender-appropriate colours'); (iii) respond differently to girls' and boys' moods, displays of anger and aggressive behaviour; (iv) assign chores in accordance with the child's presumed sex and gender combination: domestic chores for girls and maintenance/strength-requiring chores for boys and (v) constantly remind their child of the gender-appropriate behaviour (such as 'girls do not curse' and 'boys do not cry').[66] In addition to their direct relation with their significant others, children also form an opinion on gender roles by observing the manners in which their significant others do gender as well as by hearing other persons' stated gender beliefs.[67]

61 *Ibid*, p. 17.
62 Hunter College Women's Studies Collective, p. 171.
63 *Ibid*.
64 *Ibid*, p. 140.
65 Kramer defines significant others as people with whom the child has regular and frequent contact, who have control over rewards and punishments for the child and who have some image of what the child should become (Kramer, pp. 56–57).
66 These issues are commonly treated in the relevant literature. See, for example, Hunter College Women's Studies Collective, p. 140; Stockard, p. 217 and Duesterhaus, Grauerholz, Weichsel and Guittar, p. 187.
67 Kramer, p. 57.

Significant others are powerful socializing agents, but societal gender expectations are also communicated in a number of other ways. The two main communication channels are peers and cultural/commercial products.

Long before children understand the nature of religious groups, occupations or schooling, they realize that there are two sex groups and that they belong to one of these groups.[68] Infants can differentiate women from men as early as 6–9 months and toddlers can distinguish, both verbally and nonverbally, between genders by 18–24 months.[69] Children can identify themselves as girls or boys by 27 months or earlier.[70] Children learn to stereotype quickly[71] and apply these stereotypes rigorously. They rigidly expect specific traits or behaviours from gender categories[72] and apply more extensive and apparent sanctions for violating such rules when compared to adults.[73] Accordingly, peers constitute a significant gender socialization vehicle for children. They learn the commonly accepted gender-appropriate characteristics and the importance to comply with such characteristics as well as the negative implications of failing to do so from their peers.

Cultural and commercial products, such as TV shows, books, clothing, toys and even fairy tales, also operate as powerful socializing agents.[74] The influence of these different products may even constrain the influence of significant others.[75] Marketing techniques target ever younger age groups and influence how children make their decisions about whether or how to use toys and other objects they incorporate in their play.[76]

Toy decisions, which may *prima facie* be considered as having a minor impact, contribute in a significant manner in the formation of a child's general perception of the world and societal roles. First, children may perceive their toys as an 'idol' and try to imitate the characteristics represented by the toy. For instance, when two sex-segregated children soccer teams attended a special ceremony, girl participants asserted Barbie as a symbol of girl athletes.[77] It can safely be stated that the girls concerned, and a great number of girls all over the world, closely associated the Barbie doll with the 'feminine' gender. Second, the intrinsic features of the toy can create and

---

68 Stockard, p. 215.
69 Betz, Ramsey and Sekaquaptewa, p. 433.
70 *Ibid.*
71 *Ibid.*
72 *Ibid*, p. 434.
73 Stockard, p. 221.
74 Hunter College Women's Studies Collective, pp. 139–140.
75 Kramer, p. 58.
76 *Ibid.*
77 *Ibid*, p. 66.

reinforce certain gender-appropriate characteristics. For example, in 2000, Mattel designed 'the Hot Wheels computer' for boys and 'the Barbie computer' for girls. While the Hot Wheels computer contained educational software (including a human anatomy program, a logical thinking game and a mathematics program), the Barbie computer offered a more 'girly' variety consisting of miscellaneous Barbie programs (such as fashion designer and detective Barbie). According to Mattel, the problem was due to the fact that the popular Barbie software did not leave enough space on the Barbie model to include all the educational software available on the Hot Wheels model.[78] It is, however, interesting to observe that the choice of the software reflects and reinforces a popular stereotypical trait: men are better than women in science and mathematics.[79]

The stereotyping messages that children encounter in their daily lives have a great deal of significance. The messages concerned may lead to, for instance, development of some potentials and inhibition of some abilities. A child may seek to overcome a deficiency (like a muscular weakness in a boy) because it is generally considered as gender-inappropriate. On the other hand, a child may make no effort to overcome his/her gender-appropriate deficiencies and may even be proud of them. In the same vein, potential abilities seen as gender-inappropriate may not be developed at all and be eventually lost.[80]

Although most effective during the early years,[81] gender socialization is a process that incessantly continues throughout an individual's life. The institutions which the individual attends for work or study purposes, their colleagues/friends/families and, last but not least, cultural norms of the society all steadily set gendered norms and send gendered messages. This relentless flow of reminders is the key to the success of gender socialization, which constitutes the most effective method of social control: by embedding gender-appropriate behaviour in the individual's way of life, it causes the individual to regulate and to police his/her own behaviour on a permanent basis.[82] The individual thus becomes a product of the society in which he/she lives.

These observations clearly do not indicate that individuals are simple 'machines' exclusively acting on the basis of the socially imposed norms. Undoubtedly, personal agency – or, less technically put, free will – exercises

---

78 *Ibid*, p. 59.
79 On this issue, see Betz, Ramsey and Sekaquaptewa, pp. 428–429.
80 Kramer, p. 59.
81 *Ibid*, p. 57.
82 *Ibid*, p. 56.

a significant influence on individual decisions. However, who individuals are, what they want and what they choose to do all are determined to a certain extent by the gender stereotypes of the society they live in. This is due to several reasons. First, a child's taste and abilities are usually formed in accordance with gender stereotypes at a very early age. Some interests and abilities may simply be oppressed and thereby be lost due to their non-compliance with common beliefs on gender-appropriate behaviour. Second, not abiding by social constructs is generally not a simple matter of choice.[83] Social constructs feel very natural, real and at the same time unavoidable and inescapable.[84] Accordingly, individuals may not even question some typical gender characteristics, and even when they do, they may feel that such characteristics are inescapable. Third, research shows that one does not have to endorse a given stereotype in order to be affected by its implications: one needs only be aware that others may endorse it.[85] Last but not least, individuals opting not to comply with their 'appropriate' stereotype have to deal with the social reactions to their decisions.[86]

Gender stereotypes provide marketers with an ideal tool by amplifying the relatively minor biological differences between the sexes. To convince consumers that they need products and services that are specifically engineered for their gender, producers merely need to tap into these social constructs. Most consumers literally 'buy into' this essentialist-based marketing stating that men and women are different and thereby they need different products.[87] Marketers also seem to have successfully convinced both women and men that the gendered products available on the market are in fact different, not only by their design but also by their ingredients and functionality (e.g. products that are more adapted for pH levels, hormones, personal care etc.).[88] As a matter of fact, most consumers, and not just women, opt for items that 'match' their gender, regardless of their price.[89]

D.2.2 Gendered products: not always pink and tiny

In a study they conducted, Tilburg, Lieven, Herrmann and Townsend established that the purchase intent of consumers varied significantly in correlation with the 'gender level' of a product. As per their study, on a point scale

83 May, pp. 7–8.
84 *Ibid.*
85 Betz, Ramsey, Sekaquaptewa, p. 429.
86 Kramer, p. 75.
87 Duesterhaus, Grauerholz, Weichsel and Guittar, p. 187.
88 *Ibid.*
89 *Ibid.*

that varied from 2.54 to 2.85, the purchase intent of gender-undifferentiated products equalled 2.54, whereas it amounted to 2.69 for masculine products and to 2.77 for feminine products.[90]

This 'higher appeal' can be explained by the following process: (i) products that are strongly gendered elicit a more positive affective attitude in consumers than those that are less gendered due to the easy processing of the stimuli;[91] (ii) this positive affective attitude results in a higher perception of the aesthetic value;[92] (iii) high aesthetics suggest better functionality[93] and (iv) a product that is perceived to be more functional is sold more easily.

This phenomenon has a parallel in the social psychology literature: 'beautiful is good'.[94] It has been observed that people perceived to be beautiful are assumed to carry the other socially desirable characteristics, such as intelligence, competence at one's job and ethical behaviour.[95] Similarly, a product that is perceived to be 'beautiful', which is the case of the gendered products, is assumed to bear the other desirable characteristics that may be expected from a product.

Consequently, to maximize their sales, manufacturers tend to 'genderize' their products as much as possible. Since the 'gender' of a product is mainly determined by its aesthetics, i.e. physical appearance, the determinant factor in the genderization process is the design of the product.

The genderization thereby occurs by means of the colour, the material and the shape of the product. The colour of a product carries the potential to evoke certain emotional and psychological responses.[96] Colours are thus carefully chosen and used not only on the product itself but also in its advertising, packaging, logo design etc. Products with lighter tones, more colours or a shiny reflectiveness enhance the perception of a product's femininity. On the other hand, products with darker tones, fewer colours or a dim reflectiveness enhance the perception of a product's masculinity.[97]

The shape and the material of a product play a role that is as significant as the colour in the genderization process. A slim proportion, round shape or curvy lines enhances the perception of a product's femininity, whereas a bulky proportion, angular shape or straight lines enhance the perception of

---

90 Tilburg, Lieven, Herrmann and Townsend, p. 435.
91 *Ibid*, pp. 426–427.
92 *Ibid*, p. 426.
93 *Ibid*.
94 *Ibid*.
95 *Ibid*.
96 *Ibid*, p. 424.
97 *Ibid*.

a product's masculinity.[98] In the same vein, products that appear to have a smooth texture, soft surface or light weight are perceived to be more 'feminine', while products that appear to have a rough texture, hard surface or heavy weight are perceived to be more 'masculine'.[99]

Genderization is thus obtained not only by means of 'pinking and shrinking' a product but also by a great variety of other methods. Products that we use are specifically designed to be gendered. Pink products constitute only the tip of the 'gendered products' iceberg.

D.2.3 *Physical appearance: the ultimate way of doing gender*

Individuals perform and signal their gender on a continuous basis. The ultimate way to do gender is adopting a gender-appropriate physical appearance (clothing, hair style, way of talking, way of walking and other similar external characteristics).

Physical appearance of women and men has traditionally been a popular and important subject. For instance, two 17th-century British pamphlets debated proper behaviour and proper attire for both sexes.[100] The modern version of such pamphlets may be observed in regulations relating to physical attire for students and employees. Most institutions closely monitor their affiliates' use of accessories, cosmetics, jewellery, clothing, tattoos and piercings. A comprehensive dress code regulation example is the Corporate Wear Guidelines of the UBS,[101] a Swiss bank.

Between the two sexes, the physical appearance of the female sex has certainly been subject to more debate and more severe criticism. This tendency is quite apparent and may be noticed by the sole observation of fashion

---

98 *Ibid.*
99 *Ibid.*
100 Case, pp. 24–25. The British pamphlets concerned are cited by Case in the following manner: HIC-MULIER: OR, THE MAN-WOMAN: BEING A MEDECINE TO CURE THE COLTISH DISEASE OF THE STAGGERS IN THE MASCULINE-FEMININES OF OUR TIMES, EXPREST IN A BRIEF DECLAMATION, 1620, reprinted by The Scholar Press Limited in 1973 and HAEC-VIR: OR, THE WOMANISH-MAN: BEING AN ANSWERE TO A LATE BOOKE INTITULATED HIC-MULIER, EXPREST IN A BRIEFE DIALOGUE BETWEENE HAEC-VIR THE WOMANISH-MAN, AND HIC-MULIER THE MAN-WOMAN, 1620, reprinted by the Scholar Press Limited in 1973.
101 The UBS dress code is a very popular example which also formed the subject of a number of newspaper articles. The full version of the dress code can be consulted on the following link: https://static1.squarespace.com/static/55e0c62fe4b096b6619ff3d9/t/571bde1907 eaa0d2558be4f6/1461444174809/Ubs+Dress+Code+English+2010.pdf [last accessed on 21 February 2018].

magazines available on the market. It can, however, also be deducted from more official documents, such as pamphlets distributed by governments and court decisions. For instance, when a few women in London adopted a slightly masculine dress code in the early 17th century, pamphlets framing them as 'men-women' were immediately distributed and the preachers were instructed to preach against the practice.[102] Another example is the *Price Waterhouse v. Hopkins* decision,[103] rendered by the US Supreme Court, which discusses a case where a female employee's partnership application was put on hold because she failed to "walk femininely, talk femininely, dress femininely, wear make-up, have her hair styled, and wear jewellery".[104,105]

Not all reactions are so severe, but such reactions do exist, albeit in different forms. Physical appearance thus constitutes a significant source of social power, or in some cases powerlessness. Not only the social acceptance but also the success of an individual depends on it. Regular research studies have shown that there is a strong link between physical appearance and success. It was proven that this holds especially true for women: the findings report that women's physical appearance is more pertinent for their achievements when compared to men.[106]

Doing gender by means of physical appearance also bears a significant psychological importance. Through the purchase of a deodorant with floral fragrance or the obtainment of a 'feminine' haircut, women are able to express themselves as 'feminine' in a largely 'masculine' world.[107] Products and services that are linked personally and/or biologically to the body allow women to participate in women's culture.[108] Haircuts, through which women 'do gender', constitute a typical service of this kind.[109]

The critical role of appearance is constantly felt by women, by means of fashion magazines, their peers, marketing strategies, TV shows and other similar social and cultural vehicles. Marketing strategies, aimed at sales of goods and services, are persuasive because they are known to reflect the dominant views of the society.[110] Women also feel the psychological need

102 Wiesner, p. 253.
103 *Price Waterhouse v. Hopkins*, 490 U.S. 228 (1989).
104 *Ibid*, p. 235.
105 The Court held that the approach followed by the employees of the organization in the *Hopkins* case amounted to an impermissible sex-stereotyping.
106 Kramer, pp. 71–72.
107 Duesterhaus, Grauerholz, Weichsel and Guittar, p. 185.
108 *Ibid*.
109 *Ibid*.
110 Kramer, pp. 71–72.

to participate in women's culture as much as possible. It seems clear that the over-pricing of 'feminine' products and services aims to exploit these common tendencies.

E Inescapable prison of the sex-based pink tax

The pink tax is not an amount paid due to lack of self-control. It is not an amount paid by deliberate choice. It is not an amount paid to purchase the symbols of a certain lifestyle. It cannot be avoided by being reasonably attentive. It cannot be avoided by becoming a 'market maven'. It cannot be avoided without facing social, economic and psychological repercussions. It is an inescapable sex-based prison.

The pink tax is due on a number of products and services of all price ranges designed for women. It does not only cover luxurious products and services. Even the most mundane products and services are tainted by it. Women of all lifestyles suffer from it.

The pink tax is not only due on pink products. It can be levied on all gendered products targeting women. Almost all products on the market are strongly gendered. Neither women nor men can refrain from buying gendered products, which are carefully designed to reflect the preferences of the targeted sex in an extremely subtle manner. Genderization of a product oftentimes goes undetected by the target group. Avoiding the purchase of any gendered product is an unattainable aim. Trying to avoiding the pink tax by refraining from purchasing any gendered product is an elusive dream.

The pink tax cannot be avoided by purchasing men's products. No human being can be forced to wear clothing items that do not fit his/her size. No human being can be compelled to smell in a way he/she does not like. No child can be constrained to play with toys specifically designated for a sex that is not his/hers and to suffer the rigid sanctions coming from his/her peers because of it.

The pink tax is levied on some services rendered to women. The price disparity exists before the extra amounts charged for additional costs incurred due to the difficulties encountered in rendering such services. The price differences exist on the sole basis of sex. Women do not get the option to order a 'men's service' and thereby to pay the 'men's price', even when they opt for services that are completely identical to the ones provided to men. Avoiding the pink tax on services is a futile endeavour.

The pink tax does not only concern 'feminine females'. It concerns all females: androgynous, feminine or masculine. It concerns the female sex. It concerns all women wearing a white shirt, taking her clothes to a dry-cleaner and getting a haircut (even if it is a men's model) in a hairdresser.

The pink tax is a women's prison created by the market. It cannot be escaped from by individual efforts. It can be escaped from only to a certain degree by collective efforts.[111] There exists, however, one way out: government intervention. The question is, will it ever materialize?

F To perpetuate or to end, that is the only question

No market is genuinely free. Quite the opposite: even the most 'free' markets are heavily regulated by governments. Markets merely look 'free' due to unconditional acceptance of the underlying regulations, which causes individuals to fail to notice them in their daily lives.[112]

Ground rules imposed by governments upon markets include tradable products and services (e.g. restriction on sales of firearms), licenses and conditions required to perform some services and to commercialize certain products (such as a lawyer's licence and shares tradable on the stockmarket), conditions of trade (for instance, product liability and consequences of a delivery failure), price regulations (like rent controls and interest rates on loans)[113] and regulations relating to the inner dynamics of the market (for example, restrictions imposed by competition law and consumer law). These sets of rules are not based on a purely economic logic. Most of the time, they are not based on science, either. Yet they are always determined by political decisions.[114]

As per the predominant opinion, markets should be as free as possible and governments should intervene as scarcely as possible. What should be the limits of a given market's freedom, however, is subjective. It lies in the eyes of beholders.[115] Interdiction of slavery, interdiction of child labour and all environmental regulations, which seem innate today, were all argued to constitute a restriction to the free market policy at some point (not necessarily very far back) in history. For instance, when the strict child labour regulations were introduced in Europe and North America in the late 19th

111 Persistent social reaction may cause some producers to eliminate the pink tax levied on the services and/or products that they provide. For instance, Tesco (a British multinational grocery) opted for reducing the price of pink razors by half to bring it in line with their male counterpart. Tesco was charging £1 for a pack of women's razors, while a pack of men's razors cost £0.50 (in *Mirror*, Ruki Sayid, "Pink Tax Slashed as Tesco Cuts Price of Women's Razors to the Same as Men's", available on the following link: www.mirror.co.uk/news/uk-news/pink-tax-slashed-tesco-cuts-9550279 [last accessed on 21 February 2018]).
112 Chang, *23 Things*, pp. 1 and 4.
113 *Ibid*, pp. 4–5.
114 Chang, *Economics*, p. 395.
115 Chang, *23 Things*, p. 2.

to early 20th centuries, the opponents argued that child labour did not cause a problem in the first place: children wanted to work and company owners wanted to hire them.[116] On the other hand, for the proponents of the regulations, the right of children not to have to work simply weighed more than the right of factory owners to hire workers as profitably as possible.[117]

The contours of the free market are thus designated by subjective opinions deriving from politics. As a matter of fact, in every case where free market proponents argue that a certain regulation should not be introduced because it would restrict the 'freedom' of a certain market, they are not stating an objective economic truth: they are merely stating their political opinion about the rights that are to be defended by the proposed law.[118] They are merely insinuating that the right in question does not weigh as much as the right of producers to maximize their profits.

Arguing that governments should not intervene on the pink tax amounts to stating that the right of female consumers to be treated equally to male consumers weighs less than the right of producers to maximize their profits. It suggests that concealing the payment of the pink tax by reducing the amount of product contained in a package and displaying the same price tag as the product's 'male counterpart', instead of clearly indicating the price difference on the price tag, is any different than misleading the consumers by false advertising or insufficient information (which are regulated in details). It implies that offering discounts or free services uniquely to male consumers is acceptable. It advocates that women should be charged an additional amount for being women. It makes a political statement.

Such a statement is untenable due to one simple fact: women are showing a strong reaction to the practice of gender-pricing. To raise awareness on the issue, women's rights organizations are creating projects,[119] newspapers and magazines are frequently publishing articles and TV programs (mostly news programs) discuss the problem from time to time. The more awareness is raised, the stronger the reaction becomes. A robust social mobilization leading to a change does not seem very far away. As a matter of fact, the

---

116 *Ibid*, pp. 2–3.
117 *Ibid*, p. 3.
118 *Ibid*, p. 10.
119 To raise awareness, GIRLTALKHQ (The Global Headquarters of Female Empowerment News Media) conducted a project with a local coffee shop in Toronto, Canada. The coffee shop displayed two different coffee prices (men and women) and charged women more than men for a day. More information on the project is available on GIRLTALKHQ's website (http://girltalkhq.com/fightpinktax/#learn_more [last accessed on 21 February 2018]). This experiment is also discussed further in Chapter V, Subsection E.2, titled "Pink tax is a fully hidden tax".

main factors driving social mobilization are all present: one's identity as a woman is associated with a disadvantage (i.e. paying an additional amount for no justifiable reason), group boundaries are impermeable (women cannot generally become men) and structural gender relations are seen as illegitimate (paying an additional amount on the sole basis of sex is perceived to be unfair).[120] Accordingly, it seems that governments will have to intervene anyway, if not on their own initiative then due to social pressure. Most importantly, such a statement endorses the violation of applicable laws.[121] The pink tax is unlawful. Governments do not only need to but also have to intervene.

The pink tax cannot be perpetuated. It needs to come to an end.

Bibliography

Books and academic articles

Batalha Luisa and Reynolds Katherine J., Gender and Personality: Beyond Gender Stereotypes to Social Identity and the Dynamics of Social Change, in Ryan Michelle K. and Branscombe Nyla R. (eds), *The SAGE Handbook of Gender and Psychology*, Sage Publications, 2013.

Best Deborah L., Gender Stereotypes, in Ember Carol R. and Ember Melvin (eds), *Encyclopedia of Sex and Gender, Men and Women in the World's Cultures*, Volume 1, Kluwer Academic/Plenum Publishers, 2004.

Betz Diana E., Ramsey Laura R. and Sekaquaptewa Denise, Gender Stereotype Threat among Women and Girls, in Ryan Michelle K. and Branscombe Nyla R. (eds), *The SAGE Handbook of Gender and Psychology*, Sage Publications, 2013.

Chang Ha-Joon, *Economics: The User's Guide*, A Pelican Introduction, Pelican Books, Penguin Group, 2014 (cited as: Economics).

Chang Ha-Joon, *23 Things They Don't Tell You About Capitalism*, Penguin Books, Penguin Group, 2011 (cited as: 23 Things).

Dobelli Rolf, The Art of Thinking Clearly, Sceptre, Hodder & Stoughton, 2013.

Duesterhaus Megan, Grauerholz Liz, Weichsel Rebecca and Guittar Nicholas A., The Cost of Doing Femininity: Gendered Disparities in Pricing of Personal Care Products and Services, *Gender Issues*, Issue 28, 2011, pp. 175–191.

Gladwell Malcolm, *The Tipping Point, How Little Things Can Make a Big Difference*, Back Bay Books, 2000.

Hunter College Women's Studies Collective, *Women's Realities, Women's Choices*, Oxford University Press, 1995.

Kramer Laura, *The Sociology of Gender, A Brief Introduction*, 2nd edition, Roxbury Publishing Company, 2005.

120 On social mobilization, see Batalha and Reynolds, pp. 178–179.
121 On this point see Chapter VII, titled "Government Intervention".

Listen-Heyes Catherine and Neokleous Elena, Gender-Based Pricing in the Hairdressing Industry, *Journal of Consumer Policy*, Volume 23, Issue 2, 2000, pp. 107–126.

May Vanessa, Introducing a Sociology of Personal Life, in May Vanessa (ed), *Sociology of Personal Life*, Palgrave Macmillan, 2011.

Mischel Walter, *The Marshmallow Test*, Bantam Press, 2014.

Segal Edwin S., Cultural Constructions of Gender, in Ember Carol R./Ember Melvin (eds), *Encyclopedia of Sex and Gender, Men and Women in the World's Cultures*, Volume 1, Kluwer Academic/Plenum Publishers, 2004.

Southerton Dale, Consumer Culture and Personal Life, in May Vanessa (ed), *Sociology of Personal Life*, Palgrave Macmillan, 2011.

Thaler Richard H., *Misbehaving, The Making of Behavioural Economics*, Penguin Books, Penguin Random House, 2016.

Tilburg Miriam van, Lieven Theo, Herrmann Andreas and Townsend Claudia, Beyond 'Pink It and Shrink It' Perceived Product Gender, Aesthetics, and Product Evaluation, *Psychology and Marketing*, Volume 32, Issue 4, Wiley Periodicals, 2015, pp. 422–437.

Wiesner Merry E., *Women and Gender in Early Modern Europe, New approaches to European history*, Cambridge University Press, 1993.

Studies and reviews

Guidance on the Use of Gender in Pricing of Goods and Services, The Office of the Attorney General and the Human Rights Commission, State of Vermont, June 2016, available on the following link: http://hrc.vermont.gov/sites/hrc/files/gender-based%20pricing%20guidance.pdf [last accessed on 12 February 2018] (cited as Guidance on Gender-Based Pricing, State of Vermont).

From Cradle to Cane: The Cost of Being a Female Consumer, New York City Department of Consumer Affairs, December 2015, available on the following link: https://www1.nyc.gov/assets/dca/downloads/pdf/partners/Study-of-Gender-Pricing-in-NYC.pdf [last accessed on 16 February 2018] (cited as From Cradle to Cane).

109 *Harvard Law Review*, 1995–1996, pp. 1839–1844 (cited as Harvard Law Review).

5 The pink tax

The Schrödinger's cat of tax law

The concept of 'pink tax' is comparable to Schrödinger's cat[1] for the purposes of tax law: the box is yet to be opened to observe whether the cat is alive or dead. In other words, no analysis from a tax law perspective has been made up to this date[2] to determine whether the 'pink tax' is effectively a 'tax' despite being labelled that way. This chapter conducts the experiment. To this end, first the concept of 'tax' is defined in its general traits and to the extent relevant for the purposes of the analysis being conducted in this book (A). Second, the concept of 'consumption tax' is briefly laid out (B). Third, the concept of 'hidden tax' is succinctly described (C). To conclude, the pink tax is examined in the light of the definitions given (D).

---

1 'Schrödinger's cat' is a popular thought experiment put forward by the Nobel-prize winning physicist Edwin Schrödinger. The experiment concerned consists of placing a cat in a windowless steel box along with a Geiger counter attached to a hammer, a vial of poison and a radioactive substance. If the radioactive substance decays, the Geiger counter detects it and triggers the hammer, which in turn smashes the vial containing the poison, killing, thereby, the cat. The radioactive decay is a random process, and it is not possible to predict whether or when it will happen. Accordingly, until the box is opened, there is no way for the observer to know whether the cat is alive or dead. In other words, until the observation is made the cat is simultaneously alive and dead. Although not relevant for the purposes of this book, it is important to underline that popular culture somewhat distorted the meaning and the true purpose of the experiment. In fact, Schrödinger put this thought experiment forward to express his disagreement with the Copenhagen Interpretation of quantum mechanics, which essentially states that an object in a physical system can simultaneously exist in all possible configurations, but observation forces the system to collapse and the object to be in just one of those possible states. According to the physicist such an interpretation is untenable, since it would, for instance, imply that a cat can simultaneously be alive and dead, which is simply not possible.

2 February 2018.

A Definition of 'tax'

The notion of 'tax' is not immutable. Both the concept of tax and its functionalities have changed across time, depending on several factors, like the relations between the state and the individual.[3] 'Tax' was first conceived of as a levy imposed by the monarch.[4] Around the 16th century it evolved into a levy in exchange for a service provided by the state with the consent of the citizens' representatives.[5] Finally, it has taken the form of "a compulsory and unconditional levy, based on the ability to pay and not in exchange for services received".[6] This latter conception constitutes the current form of 'tax'.

The concept of 'tax' does not seem to diverge from country to country in a significant manner. Although different countries may stress different elements of taxation, the fundamental notion of tax remains the same.[7] Accordingly, main characteristics of taxes may be identified by means of examining some of the definitions and explanations given by scholars and international organizations in the light of their comparative studies.

Adams defines 'tax' as a 'forced exaction'. He states that "A tax is owed because a government orders it to be paid. Nothing else is required".[8] Silverman defines 'tax' by distinguishing it from price. He indicates that "[a] tax is not a price, but a compulsory exaction in which there is no *quid pro quo* element".[9] In the same vein, the OECD's working definition of 'tax' is "a compulsory unrequited payment to the government".[10] Similarly, Thuronyi defines 'tax' as "a required payment to the government".[11] The author underlines the fact that this definition is both under- and over-inclusive: under-inclusive since taxes may also be paid to government-controlled entities and not exclusively to the government itself,[12] and over-inclusive since the term 'tax' does not comprise civil or criminal fines.[13] A comparable definition is also provided by the IBFD International Tax Glossary, which indicates that a tax is "a government levy which is not in return for a

---

3 Barassi, p. 59.
4 *Ibid.*
5 *Ibid*, pp. 59–60.
6 *Ibid*, p. 60.
7 *Ibid*, p. 64.
8 Adams, p. 1.
9 Silverman, p. 66.
10 www.oecd.org/ctp/glossaryoftaxterms.htm#T [last accessed on 22 February 2018].
11 Thuronyi, p. 45.
12 *Ibid.*
13 *Ibid.*

specific benefit and is not imposed by way of fine or penalty (e.g. for non-compliance with the law), except in some cases where related to tax-related offences".[14]

More specifically, 'tax' is the most important category of 'compulsory contributions'[15] that may be defined as monetary contributions unilaterally imposed under public law which serve (at least partly) to raise revenues and are payable to public authorities.[16] Compulsory contributions are generally subdivided into fees, special contributions and taxes.[17] Fees can be described as compulsory contributions paid by the beneficiaries of public services.[18] Special contributions consist of compulsory contributions linked to the contributor's receipt of a benefit as a result of the carrying out of public works or the establishment or expansion of public services (like sidewalk improvements).[19] Finally, "[t]ax is the residual category of compulsory contributions where the taxpayer does not receive anything in return for the payment".[20]

In the light of these different definitions, the main characteristics of taxes may be established as follows:

1 **Compulsory**. "Taxes are required from taxpayers without their individual consent".[21] Once the taxable event occurs, taxpayers are under the obligation to pay the tax. They are not given the choice of abstaining from the payment.

2 **Unrequited**. Taxpayers do not receive any specific benefits in return for their payment of the tax.

3 **Deriving from public law**. Taxes are regulated by public law.

4 **Payable to a government or to a government-controlled entity**. Taxes are collected either by an organ of the government or by a government-controlled entity.

5 **The main aim is to raise revenues**. Although, traditionally, the main aim of taxes is to raise revenues for government expenses, other political, social and economic aims may also be relevant.[22] It is possible to state that taxes are due in order to allow the government to promote

---

14 IBFD International Tax Glossary, p. 416.
15 Barassi, p. 60.
16 Ferdinand Kirchhof, *Grundriss des Abgabenrechts 1* (1991), cited by Thuronyi, p. 48.
17 Thuronyi, p. 48.
18 *Ibid*.
19 *Ibid*, p. 49.
20 *Ibid*.
21 Bourgeois, p. 159.
22 Barassi, p. 64.

the interests that are considered to be the general interests of the state (such as redistribution of wealth and income and directing consumer's choices).[23] In a nutshell, taxes are imposed for public purposes.[24]

To be characterized as a tax, the levy concerned should fulfil all these conditions in a **cumulative** manner.

B Concept of 'consumption tax'

Consumption tax may be defined as "[a] tax whose base is expenditure on consumption rather than income".[25] Consumption taxes are traditionally regrouped into two main categories: general and selective.

A general consumption tax is levied on the majority of available goods and services by means of an equal rate or a limited number of different rates. In principle, a number of goods and services, most commonly health care and educational services, are tax exempt. Also, the basic necessities of life generally benefit from reduced rates. The VAT and the GST are examples of general consumption taxes.

A selective consumption tax targets only **specific** goods and services, thereby allowing a government to discriminate between commodities and impose a variety of different tax rates. Due to their discriminatory nature, selective consumption taxes are distortionary by definition.[26] Selective consumption taxes are levied as a fixed amount per item sold (e.g. $1 per item) or on an *ad valorem* basis. The *ad valorem* tax is calculated as a percentage of the retail sales price. Some products, like cigarettes, may be targeted by both on a fixed amount and on an *ad valorem* basis.[27]

The objectives of selective consumption taxes include, but are not limited to, discouraging undesired consumption and taxing luxury goods to ensure a more efficient redistribution of wealth. Selective taxes whose main purpose is to discourage the consumption of a particular product rather than to raise revenue are commonly referred to as 'sin taxes'.

The most widely recognized examples of sin taxes are taxes levied on alcoholic beverages and tobacco products. Recently, a variety of taxes to tackle obesity, most commonly the 'sugar tax' (or 'soda tax') and 'fat tax' (or 'fast food tax'), have also emerged. The sugar tax and/or fat tax are

---

23 *Ibid.*
24 *Ibid.*
25 IBFD International Tax Glossary, p. 93.
26 Vermeend, Ploeg and Timmer, p. 195.
27 *Ibid*, p. 210.

currently levied in a number of countries, such as India, Denmark, Mexico and the UK,[28] and are likely to be introduced in a number of other countries, like Ghana.[29]

Studies conducted on the matter show that sin taxes efficiently discourage the consumption of the targeted products. For example, it was proven that alcohol taxes are fairly effective in discouraging drinking, especially for younger drinkers.[30] Similarly, it was reported that in Mexico, a one peso per litre (app. €0.05) tax on sugary drinks, introduced in the beginning of 2014, successfully diminished the demand of such drinks by 6%.[31] In the same vein, the Danish tax on saturated fat, which was abolished in 2013 due to significant administrative burdens it had caused, decreased the consumption of the products containing saturated fat, such as butter and margarine, by 10% to 15%.[32]

C Concept of 'hidden tax'

The concept of 'hidden tax' cannot be defined with precision. This is mainly due to the fact that hidden tax constitutes a largely political and popular notion.[33] It is thereby subject to a great variety of divergent interpretations, depending on the point that needs to be made in a given debate. There seems to be, however, a general consensus on the fact that a hidden tax is a tax that "people pay without realizing they are being taxed".[34] In fact, both the IBFD International Tax Glossary and the OECD Glossary of Tax Terms loosely define the term 'hidden tax' as an indirect tax[35] paid by the consumer without his/her knowledge.[36]

---

28 'Soft Drinks Industry Levy', introduced as of April 2018.
29 On 11 January 2018, the Ghanaian Government proposed the imposition of a 'health tax' on the consumption of sugar and cigarettes [IBFD Tax News, 22 January 2018].
30 Vermeend, Ploeg and Timmer, p. 195.
31 In *The Times*, Alan Caulfield, "Noonan Opens Door for Sugar Tax on Drinks", available on the following link: www.thetimes.co.uk/tto/irishnews/article4673565.ece [last accessed on 22 February 2018].
32 Jensen and Smed, p. 25.
33 On this point see Kornhauser, p. 332.
34 *Ibid.*
35 There does not exist a generally accepted distinction between a direct and an indirect tax. There is, however, a fair amount of consensus that the income tax is a direct tax and taxes on consumption (such as a VAT, sales tax and excise duties) are generally, but not necessarily, indirect taxes.
36 IBFD International Tax Glossary, p. 218; OECD Glossary of Tax Terms, available online on the following link: www.oecd.org/ctp/glossaryoftaxterms.htm#H [last accessed on 22 February 2018].

The ambiguousness of the term 'hidden tax' primarily resides in establishing the relevant level of the general public knowledge that may be considered as sufficient for a tax to be deemed transparent. Thereupon, the main concern is to fix an appropriate threshold of 'necessary knowledge'. In other words, the difficulty lies in determining how well a tax needs to be concealed to be characterized as a hidden tax.[37]

C.1 The necessary level of concealment for a tax to be considered as 'hidden'

Depending on the level of taxpayers' lack of knowledge, a hidden tax can be qualified as 'partially' or 'fully' hidden. The former is a tax that is known or easily knowable but hidden from the taxpayer's direct view.[38] The latter consists of taxes of which the ultimate incidence may only be determined by experts and, therefore, are not known or easily knowable by the general public.[39]

For instance, it may be argued that when the retail prices are VAT-inclusive, which is the case in the EU, VAT becomes a partially hidden tax. In such cases, a good or a service is directly advertised as costing, for instance, 115 Euros (100 Euros for the good/service + 15 Euros in VAT) and consumers pay the advertised price without readily grasping that they are paying 15 Euros of VAT at the moment of purchase. Nonetheless, consumers are aware of the fact that they are paying the VAT, and they can determine the amount concerned in a rather straightforward manner: by taking a look at the cash register receipt. In contrast, consumers are generally subject to a fully hidden tax in cases where a good or a service is exempt from VAT. In fact, when a particular good or service is exempt from VAT, its supplier is usually not entitled to deduct the input VAT, i.e. the VAT reimbursed by the supplier concerned in relation to goods and services it acquired for business purposes to produce the exempt supply. As a consequence, the non-deductible input tax forms part of the supplier's business costs and is 'hidden' in its selling prices. The consumers pay, thereby, an amount of tax without possibly detecting its existence. The experts, on the other hand, are well aware of the tax concerned.

---

37 Taxes may also be hidden by simply not being labelled as a 'tax' but as a 'fee', a 'contribution' or a similar term. This aspect will not be developed further, since it is not relevant for the purposes of this book. For more information on this point, see McCaffery and Baron, *Thinking About Tax*, pp. 10–12.
38 McCaffery and Baron, *Uncovering Hidden Taxes*, p. 1.
39 *Ibid.*

While a fully hidden tax does generally not give rise to interpretation problems, the circumstances under which a tax can be qualified as a partially hidden tax are subject to discussion. For instance, Bickley argues that VAT may be considered as a partially hidden tax, since consumers pay a small amount of VAT with each purchase and are not fully aware of the aggregate VAT paid for a year.[40] On the other hand, Riley, Schlecht and Berthoud assert that sales taxes can generally not be considered as hidden taxes, because the exact amount of the tax is clearly indicated on the cash register receipt.[41] Similarly, Riley, Schlecht and Berthoud suggest that the double taxation occurring when a company proceeds to a distribution of its income to its shareholders (i.e. the company is subject to corporate tax on the income concerned, and the shareholders are subject to income tax on their share of the very same income) is a hidden tax. [42] It can be argued that no hidden taxes arise in such a case, since the amount of both the corporate tax and the income tax are clearly known by all relevant taxpayers. The fact that the effect produced by the cumulation of the taxes (i.e. the double taxation) is ignored, should not, *per se*, be interpreted as amounting to a partially hidden tax.

Some taxes, however, are considered as partially hidden taxes in a quasi-unanimous manner. For instance, the employer's share of social security contributions is frequently cited as an example of a partially hidden tax.[43] The tax concerned effectively fulfils both criteria of a partially hidden tax: all employees are aware of the fact that their employer has to reimburse such a tax, but they are not actively involved in the payment of the sum.

It seems reasonable to argue that a tax that is not apparent for any reason should be qualified as a partially hidden tax. This refers to the cases where taxpayers are aware of the fact that the tax is due, but they either do not clearly know the exact amount before paying it (like the VAT-inclusive retail price) or they do not effectively participate in the payment of the tax concerned (like the employer's share of social security contributions). A tax, however, should not be considered as being partially hidden solely on the basis that its overall impact may be ignored by the taxpayers (such as the calculation of the aggregate VAT paid for a year and the cumulative effect of different taxes).

---

40 Bickley, p. 28.
41 Riley, Schlecht and Berthoud, p. 2.
42 *Ibid*, p. 3.
43 On this point, see, for example, McCaffery and Baron, *Uncovering Hidden Taxes*, p. 1 and Andrew Sentance, *Uncovering the Impact of Hidden Taxes on Employment*, Paying Taxes 2016, PwC Commentary, available on the following link: www.pwc.com/gx/en/paying-taxes-2016/paying-taxes-2016-uncovering-the-impact.pdf [last accessed on 22 February 2018].

C.2 Ignorance is bliss

The bounded rationality of human beings and the wide range of heuristics and biases deriving from it form the main reason for the hidden taxes' existence. Research shows that individuals do not exhibit a negative reaction to hidden taxes,[44] since they cannot, wholly or partly, grasp that they are paying the taxes concerned. This phenomenon is usually explained by the following factors:[45]

1 Ignorance: Individuals simply do not have enough information on the taxes concerned.
2 Optimism: Individuals believe that hidden taxes fall on others and not on them.
3 Isolation effect: Individuals often attend only to the information immediately before them. Accordingly, they respond to the most obviously salient aspect of an issue without considering further implications. Hidden taxes are generally concealed in such 'further implications'.
4 Low benefits: The benefits to be obtained from a comprehensive understanding of the tax system is deemed to be low by individuals who do not wish to specialize in tax.
5 Complexity of the tax system: The tax system is technical, and a widely available mechanism to educate citizens about tax does generally not exist.

As suggested by cognitive psychology and behavioural economics, "what is less known is generally less hurtful" due to the combination of heuristics and biases.[46] This implies that as long as hidden taxes remain veiled, they are not likely to attract any public opposition. Quite expectedly, when the veil is removed, this 'soothing' effect of hidden taxes substantially diminishes.[47]

The impact of hidden taxes on taxpayers can be illustrated by a number of examples. For instance, the study on toll prices conducted by the economist Finkelstein demonstrated that when tolls were collected electronically – and

44 McCaffery and Baron, *Uncovering Hidden Taxes*, p. 32.
45 On this point, see *Ibid*, pp. 2–3; McCaffery/Baron, *Thinking About Tax*, p. 7 and Klazar, p. 53.
46 McCaffery and Baron, *Uncovering Hidden Taxes*, p. 2.
47 In a study he conducted, Klazar observed that the 'soothing effect' of hidden taxes substantially diminishes when individuals are provided with the relevant information relating to the genuine features of the hidden tax [Klazar, p. 60]. See also McCaffery and Baron for other biases that may prevent individuals from reacting to a hidden tax even in cases where they are provided with sufficient level of information [McCaffery and Baron, *Uncovering Hidden Taxes*, pp. 2 and 32].

thereby somewhat beneath the notice of the toll payers – the demand for driving on toll roads was less elastic (i.e. its fluctuation in relation to the price was reduced). In fact, the survey data suggested that drivers who opted for electronic payment not only did not know their total periodic toll costs but also were not aware of the toll rate.[48] Similarly, in a study they conducted on sales in a grocery store, Chetty, Looney and Kroft observed that when the posted prices of the goods were tax-inclusive, the quantities sold were significantly lower.[49] The study reveals that consumers simply did not calculate the tax-inclusive price prior to making their purchase. Some consumers apparently would have abstained from acquiring the goods if they had taken into consideration the amount of the tax due and the final price of the items concerned. In the same vein, increases in the rate of sales tax have been relatively modest in the US (where the posted retail prices are tax-exclusive) when compared to the EU (where the posted retail prices are tax-inclusive).[50] For instance, the sales tax rate increased from 2% to 6% between the years 1933 and 2018 in West Virginia (US) (i.e. approximately 0.04 per year), whereas the VAT rate in the Netherlands increased from 12% to 21% between the years 1969 and 2018 (i.e. approximately 0.18 per year, 4.5 times greater than the rise in West Virginia).[51] This steep escalation clearly shows that hidden taxes cause a significant decrease in the public reaction towards an increase of tax rates or the creation of new taxes.

Taxpayers seem to consistently fail to notice that they are paying a tax when the tax concerned is not utterly displayed. Even a consumption tax clearly indicated in the cash register receipt does not provoke any major reactions to the extent where the posted price of the item concerned was tax-inclusive. It can, therefore, safely be stated that hidden taxes do not have any obvious opponents.[52] A tax without opponents is a powerful tool for governments.

C.3 Governments' friend, consumers' foe

Hidden taxes can lead to larger governments, *ceteris paribus*.[53] They constitute revenue sources that governments can collect more effortlessly than

48 Amy Finkelstein, E-ZTax: *Tax Salience and Tax Rates*, 4–6, National Bureau of Economic Research, Working Paper No. 12924, 2007, pp. 18–30 cited by Galle, p. 75.
49 Raj Chetty, Adam Looney and Kory Kroft, Salience and taxation: Theory and evidence, *American Economic Review* 99, pp. 1145–1177 cited by Boadway, p. 223.
50 Brederode, p. 213.
51 *Ibid.*
52 McCaffery and Baron, *Thinking About Tax*, p. 7
53 *Ibid.*

transparent taxes. This 'ease' does not uniquely derive from the absence of obvious opponents. As is asserted by a tradition in public finance economics associated with Ramsey and Mirrlees, the most efficient tax is the one imposed on inelastic behaviour,[54] i.e. behaviour that is relatively insensitive to price. Hidden taxes constitute an important tool to sustain inelastic behaviour.[55] As a matter of fact, in order to be able to adapt their behaviour in accordance with a tax (elasticity), taxpayers must first be aware of such a tax.[56] Hidden taxes reduce this awareness by diminishing tax salience. Under these circumstances, it can be stated that governments have no interest in "laying bare the hidden tax illusion".[57]

From a taxpayer point of view, hidden taxes produce mixed effects. Such taxes are revealed to be 'minimally painful'[58] when compared to transparent taxes and, thereby, produce a positive effect on taxpayers' overall happiness. This bliss, however, is purely based on an illusion. The bitter truth is hidden taxes cause the available income of individuals to diminish. This reduction may be due to either budget misallocations primarily caused by non-informed consumption decisions or covert sums deducted from individuals' income before the reception of such income by the individuals concerned.[59] Less available income implies a more limited budget to be spent on purchases. The magnitude of hidden taxes' impact on taxpayers' budgets may be as trivial as causing the individual not being able to afford a fifth spa treatment or an additional luxury item of his/her choice or as consequential as stripping him/her of the possibility to acquire some of the basic life necessities. The significance of the impact will depend on three factors:

1   The transactions, goods and services subject to hidden taxes.
2   The heaviness of the overall hidden tax burden in a given country.
3   The income level of the individual concerned: individuals of a low-income level allocate a large proportion of their income to basic necessities. Any decrease in their income is, therefore, likely to translate into a reduction of their ability to purchase essential items. As a consequence, generally, the impact of hidden taxes is more heavily felt by low-income earners.

---

54 Galle, p. 61.
55 *Ibid*, p. 62.
56 *Ibid.*
57 McCaffery and Baron, *Thinking About Tax*, p. 7
58 *Ibid*, p. 32.
59 A typical example are the taxes levied on salaries prior to their reception by employees. It can be stated that in such cases "government deceit precedes receipt'"[McCaffery and Baron, *Uncovering Hidden Taxes*, p. 1].

Hidden taxes have been revealed to be extremely useful tools to create prosperous governments and impoverished individuals. There is, however, one silver lining; both parties are 'happy' with the results: the former derive important benefits from their 'ingenious strategy', and the latter live more blissfully in their ignorance.

D Can the pink tax be qualified as a tax?

To be legally qualified as a tax, the pink tax must be: (1) compulsory, (2) unrequited, (3) mainly aimed at raising revenues, (4) payable to a government or to a government-controlled entity and (5) deriving from public law.[60] These conditions are cumulative, i.e. all conditions must be fulfilled simultaneously for a levy to constitute a tax from a legal standpoint.

D.1 The pink tax is compulsory

The pink tax is compulsory. Every time a woman purchases a product or a service subject to the pink tax, she is under the obligation to pay the tax. In fact, the finalization of her purchase simply depends upon the payment of the entire price, which includes the pink tax. She cannot complete the acquisition if she refuses to pay a certain percentage of the posted price on the basis that she would like to abstain from paying the pink tax.

As already established,[61] women cannot be reasonably expected to avoid the payment of the pink tax by refraining from buying certain products. In fact, gender-based pricing is applied to a large variety of products available on the market, and even the most mundane products are subject to it. Also, it cannot be logically argued that women must exclusively shop men's products for the sake of dodging the pink tax. Regarding the services, it is utterly clear that women cannot order men's services. These circumstances reinforce the compulsory character of the pink tax: it is mandatorily paid by all women in the course of their daily lives.

It is also important to take into consideration that some women may simply not be aware of the pink tax they reimburse. Given the fact that the amount charged as a 'pink tax' is not clearly indicated on posted prices, women may not realize that they are paying such a tax. They are also likely to have optimistic thoughts on their favourite brands and/or shops, which may lead them to consider that, unlike other women, they are not

---

60 See Section A of this chapter for more information on the main characteristics of taxes.
61 See Chapter IV, Sections D and E, titled "Underlying problem: gender-based pricing" and "Inescapable prison of the sex-based pink tax".

being charged with a pink tax. This well-concealed nature of the pink tax is another feature strengthening its compulsory character: women cannot object to the payment of a tax that is levied in a covert manner (i.e. without them realizing).

D.2 The pink tax is unrequited

The pink tax is unrequited since women do not receive a specific benefit in return for their payment of the tax. This lack of compensation should be analyzed separately for products subject to the pink tax and their service counterparts.

It is clear that, in some cases, the materials used for women's products may cost slightly more than the materials used to manufacture men's products. For example, the formula for women's deodorants may contain more expensive fragrances than those of men's.[62] It is also well-established that the price of a product is determined not only by the labour or the material necessary to manufacture it but also by other factors, such as competitor pricing, brand, country of origin, cost of production, availability of supply, cost of packaging, cost of marketing, size and method of manufacture.[63] Nonetheless, studies have showed[64] that the price disparity between women's and men's products is not exclusively due to these additional costs that may be incurred in the production and distribution processes of women's products. There exists a latent additional amount that is being charged on women's products for no justifiable reason. The end result is that women are being subjected to supplementary costs exclusively to purchase items that are substantially similar to and that will be used for the same purposes as the items bought by men. In other words, the additional cost of the pink tax is not accompanied with a specific additional benefit that may be derived by the product. In this respect, the additional amount that women have to reimburse is unrequited.

This lack of reciprocity is even more apparent in services. As already developed in detail,[65] the price disparity exists before the additional costs that may be incurred due to various factors (such as the duration, the products used and the training required to render the service) are taken into consideration. An extra amount is charged for all such costs by service

---

62 Duesterhaus, Grauerholz, Weichsel and Guittar, p. 184.
63 State of California, Bill Analysis, SB 899, p. 15.
64 On this point, see Chapter IV, Section D, titled "Underlying problem: gender-based pricing".
65 See Chapter IV, Sections D and E, titled "Underlying problem: gender-based pricing" and "Inescapable prison of sex-based pink tax".

providers on top of the initial price, which tends to be determined solely on the basis of sex. Under these circumstances, the additional cost incurred by women does not imply the provision of an additional service or an extra feature. All add-on features give rise to a supplementary charge in any case. Consequently, the additional sum paid by women commonly remains unrequited for services as well.

D.3   The main aim of the pink tax is to raise revenues . . . for private entities

There is little doubt on the fact that the pink tax is levied to raise revenues. However, the revenues raised do not, at least not directly, benefit governments. The pink tax raises revenues for private entities, i.e. enterprises manufacturing and/or commercializing the products and the services concerned. As explained earlier,[66] gender-based pricing is a by-product of the free market economy. In some industries, the prices of products/services commercialized to women are inflated in order to maximize the profits.

Thereupon, it is clear that the revenue derived from the pink tax is not used to cover government expenses or to support other political, social and economic aims. Quite the contrary: the pink tax can be qualified as a side effect of the free market economy, producing significant undesirable social and economic impacts on societies.

D.4   The pink tax is not payable to a government or to a government-controlled entity

The pink tax is entirely levied by private entities, without any government interference. Accordingly, it is clearly not payable to a government or to a government-controlled entity.

D.5   The pink tax is not regulated at all

As per the principles of legality of taxation ('*nullum tributum sine lege*') and no taxation without representation,[67] all the norms that govern the quantification and allocation of the tax burden to taxpayers must be enacted in a statute approved by the legislature,[68] which is the state organ where electors and thus taxpayers are politically represented.[69] This requirement covers the

---

66 In Chapter IV, Section D, titled "Underlying problem: gender-based pricing".
67 These two principles are usually considered as equivalents.
68 Menéndez, p. 305.
69 Bourgeois, p. 158.

taxable event, the identification of the taxpayer or passive subject as well as the tax rates.[70] It also extends to the basic norms relating to the process of tax assessment and compliance monitoring, to the extent that the norms concerned may have an impact upon the final tax to be paid or upon the basic individual rights or guarantees.[71] The importance of these two principles cannot be overstated, since they constitute a formal guarantee for taxpayers by limiting governments' discretion over tax matters, allowing taxpayers to take part in the law-making process to a certain extent and enabling taxpayers to foresee with certainty the tax implications of their activities (certainty of law).

Since the pink tax is not levied by governments or government-controlled entities, it is not regulated by tax law or – in most cases – any other laws or regulations.[72] This lack of regulation adds an extra layer of complication to the problem: not only can women consumers not foresee with certainty the exact amount of pink tax they have to pay, but also they cannot rely upon an efficient legal protection to safeguard their rights. Without rules and regulations limiting the relevant industries' discretion over pricing policies, problems incurred by the pink tax largely remain 'authorized'.

D.6 The pink tax is not a tax

The pink tax does not fulfil three of the five cumulative criteria that a tax needs to satisfy: (i) it is not payable to a government or to a government-controlled entity, (ii) it does not derive from public law and (iii) its main purpose is not to raise revenues to cover government expenses or to promote the general interests of the state. Accordingly, the pink tax cannot be qualified as a tax from a legal standpoint.

E The pink tax is economically equivalent to a tax

Although the pink tax does not fulfil all the requirements to be legally qualified as a tax, it satisfies the two criteria that produce the economic impact of taxes: being compulsory and unrequited. Consequently, even if the pink tax does not fit into the legal definition of tax, it clearly is equivalent to a tax on purely economic grounds. In fact, it is possible to state that, economically, the pink tax behaves as a **fully hidden selective consumption tax**.

---

70 Menéndez, p. 305.
71 *Ibid.*
72 This general rule suffers from some exceptions, which will be developed below in Chapter VII, titled "Government Intervention".

E.1 The pink tax is a selective consumption tax

The pink tax produces the same economic effect on taxpayers as a regular consumption tax: (i) it adds an additional cost to the price of the product/ service, (ii) the additional cost must be paid to purchase the product/service concerned and (iii) the additional cost does not provide an additional benefit to the taxpayer. In this respect, the economic effect produced by the pink tax is not any different than the economic effect produced by consumption taxes. Both are compulsory and unrequited payments made upon the purchase of a given product/service.

The pink tax should be qualified as a **selective** consumption tax, since it exclusively targets products and services meant to be consumed by women. As already mentioned,[73] selective consumption taxes are mainly levied on 'undesired products' to diminish their use (the so-called 'sin tax') and on luxury goods. It can safely be assumed that the rationale behind the pink tax is similar: an additional charge may either aim to place the product/service out of the reach of women belonging to lower-income levels or be instituted in the first place because the product/service is deemed to be 'luxurious', and, thereby, the demand is expected to be rather inelastic (i.e. the purchase occurs regardless of the price).

The purpose of levying a pink tax does not seem to be to limit the purchase of the products/services concerned by lower-income women consumers. As a matter of fact, the pink tax is due even on the most mundane products and services used by women of all income levels, such as shampoos, deodorants and haircuts. In addition, it cannot be avoided, and it is systematically due on a large variety of products and services. For the very same reasons, it cannot be argued that the rationale behind levying a pink tax is submitting 'luxury products' to tax.

The pink tax is simply a vehicle used to maximize the profits derived from the sales of the targeted items/services. Its wide scope and inevitability ensures the inelasticity of the demand: women continue to buy these items and services regardless of the fact that a higher price is being charged, since they do not have the possibility to avoid the pink tax.

The pink tax is, therefore, a selective consumption tax with an unusual aim: maximizing the profits derived from all sorts of women's products and services.

E.2 The pink tax is a fully hidden tax

The pink tax constitutes a fully hidden tax. It is not known or easily know-able by the general public, since both its existence and its amount can only

---

73 In Section B, titled "Concept of 'consumption tax'", of this chapter.

be detected by experts taking into consideration a variety of factors. Regular consumers cannot determine whether a pink tax is effectively due on an item/service that they are about to purchase. They may only assume that such a tax is due. Moreover, consumers cannot calculate the amount of the tax concerned on their own. The pink tax does not have a pre-determined rate, and it is not indicated in cash register receipts or anywhere in stores. As a matter of fact, the pink tax is designed to be well-concealed and usually remains undetected.

A project put in place in Canada by GIRLTALKHQ to draw public attention to the pink tax has shown that women and men refuse to buy products when the pink tax becomes apparent. The social experiment concerned was conducted in a coffee shop[74] in Toronto. The menu of the coffee shop was modified to include separate prices for men and women. Women's prices, written in pink, were slightly higher than men's prices (i.e. $1.50[75]), written in white. As can be seen on the video of the experiment,[76] every customer, including men, protested against the pricing policy put in place by the coffee shop. Most customers left without buying coffee. The experiment demonstrates that should the pink tax become apparent, a significant part of the population, both women and men, are likely to react to it by clearly demonstrating their opposition.

If the pink tax was not hidden, it would also be easier for women, or men buying women's products, to avoid it. A person who sees the additional pink tax amount can make an informed decision about the products and services he/she is buying and may opt for choosing another similar item/service that does not give rise to the payment of the tax. Certainly, that option would only exist to the extent where such a product or service is available on the market and the search for it would not constitute an unreasonable burden. In sectors where charging more for women's products/services is systematic, the 'quest for a pink tax-free product/service' may constitute an enormous challenge, even when the tax is not hidden.

F The cat is both alive and dead

This chapter opened the Schrödinger's box of the pink tax and discovered that the cat is both alive and dead. The pink tax does not fit into the legal definition of tax and thereby cannot legally be qualified as such. Hence,

---

74 Tokyo Smoke.
75 Canadian dollars.
76 The experiment can be viewed on the following link: http://girltalkhq.com/fightpinktax/ [last access 22 February 2018].

56   *The pink tax*

the cat is dead. On the other hand, the pink tax economically behaves like a fully hidden selective consumption tax. Thereupon, the cat is simultaneously alive.

This outcome is not very unusual from a quantum mechanics perspective. In fact, as per the 'Many-Worlds Interpretation' (the main idea of which is that there are a great number of worlds that exist in parallel at the same space and time), every time a quantum experiment with different possible outcomes is performed, all outcomes are simultaneously obtained but each outcome comes into being in a 'separate world'.[77] Individuals can only be aware of the outcome occurring in 'their' world, i.e. the world they can see. Nonetheless, all results are equally real, regardless of the fact that they do not interact with each other.

The results of the pink tax Schrödinger's cat experiment are compliant with the Many-Worlds Interpretation: in one universe (tax law) the cat is dead, whereas in another universe (economics) the cat is alive. Both results are equally real, and they do not interact with each other. In other words, tax law cannot offer a legal remedy to 'the pink tax problem', since the 'pink tax', which is not a 'real tax', does not fall within its scope.

This does not imply that there are no legal remedies available against the practice of gender-based pricing. As a matter of fact, the cat is well alive in the 'legal' universe, which **does closely interact** with the economic universe, as will be demonstrated in Chapter VII.

Bibliography

Books and academic articles

Adams Charles, *For Good and Evil: The Impact of Taxes on the Course of Civilization*, Madison Books, 2000.
Barassi Marco, The Notion of Tax and the Different Types of Taxes, in Peeters Bruno (ed), *The Concept of Tax*, EATLP International Tax Series, Volume 3, IBFD, 2005.
Bickley James M., *Value Added Tax: Concepts, Policy Issues and OECD Experiences*, Novinka Books, 2003.
Boadway Robin, *From Optimal Tax Theory to Tax Policy, Retrospective and Prospective Views*, The MIT Press, 2012.
Bourgeois Marc, Constitutional Framework of the Different Types of Income, in Peeters Bruno (ed), *The Concept of Tax*, EATLP International Tax Series, Volume 3, IBFD, 2005.

---

77 For more information on the Many-Worlds Interpretation see, for example, Stanford Encyclopedia of Philosophy, https://plato.stanford.edu/entries/qm-manyworlds/ [last accessed on 26 February 2018].

Brederode Robert F. van, VAT as a Hidden Tax: Brazil's Social Experiment, *International VAT Monitor,* IBFD, July/August 2013, pp. 213–214.

Duesterhaus Megan, Grauerholz Liz, Weichsel Rebecca and Guittar Nicholas A., The Cost of Doing Femininity: Gendered Disparities in Pricing of Personal Care Products and Services, *Gender Issues,* Issue 28, Springer, 2011, pp. 175–191.

Galle Brian D., Hidden Taxes, *Washington University Law Review,* Volume 87, 2009, pp. 59–114.

Jensen Jørgen Dejgård and Smed Sinne, The Danish Tax on Saturated Fat – Short Run Effects on Consumption, Substitution Patterns and Consumer Prices of Fats, *Food Policy,* Issue 42, Elsevier, 2013, pp. 18–31.

Klazar Stanislav, Behavioral Consequences of Optimal Tax Structure – Empirical Analysis, *European Financial and Accounting Journal,* Volume 5, 2010, pp. 51–63.

Kornhauser Marjorie E., Remembering the 'Forgotten Man' (and Woman): Hidden Taxes and the 1936 Election, in Tiley John (ed), *Studies in the History of Tax Law,* Volume 4, Hart Publishing, 2010.

McCaffery Edward J. and Baron Jonathan, Thinking About Tax, *University of Southern California Law School, Law and Economics Working Paper Series,* Paper 10, 2004 (cited as Thinking About Tax).

McCaffery Edward J. and Baron Jonathan, *Uncovering Hidden Taxes and Indirect Effects,* 2004 (cited as Uncovering Hidden Taxes), available on the following link: http://sticerd.lse.ac.uk/dps/bpde2004/McCaffery.pdf.

Menéndez Agustín José, *Justifying Taxes, Some Elements for a General Theory of Democratic Tax Law,* Kluwer Academic Publishers, 2001.

Silverman Herbert Albert, *Taxation, Its Incidence and Effects,* Palgrave Macmillan, 1931.

Thuronyi Victor, *Comparative Tax Law,* Kluwer Law International, 2003.

Vermeend Willem, Ploeg Rick van der and Timmer Jan Willem, *Taxes and the Economy: A Survey on the Impact of Taxes on Growth, Employment, Investment, Consumption and the Environment,* Edward Elgar Publishing, 2008.

Studies, reports and dictionaries

IBFD International Tax Glossary, Rogers-Glabush Julie (ed), 6th edition, IBFD, 2009 (cited as IBFD International Tax Glossary).

Riley Brian, Schlecht Eric V. and Berthoud John, *Hidden Taxes: How Much do You Really Pay?,* IPI Center for Tax Analysis, The Road Map to Tax Reform™ Series, Policy Report 160, 2001.

Sentance Andrew, *Uncovering the Impact of Hidden Taxes on Employment,* Paying Taxes 2016, PwC Commentary, available on the following link: www.pwc.com/gx/en/paying-taxes-2016/paying-taxes-2016-uncovering-the-impact.pdf [last accessed on 22 February 2018].

6   Legal analysis of the 'tampon tax'

This chapter analyzes the ongoing public debate on the second tax forming the subject matter of this book, i.e. the 'tampon tax', from a tax law perspective. To this end, first the public perception of the tampon tax is described in its general traits (A). Second, the underlying problem, i.e. consumption tax rates applied to women's sanitary protection products, is examined (B). Third, the economic impact of the tampon tax, both on an individual and on a governmental level, is assessed (C). As a result of the analysis conducted, it is concluded that the public reaction is justified (D).

A Public perception: "Crocodile meat is considered to be an essential product, whereas tampons are deemed to be luxury items"

With the slogan *"Stop taxing periods. Period."*, the fight against the tampon tax has been actively ongoing worldwide for over three years. Although the most remarkable and persistent campaign seems to have been conducted in the UK, women in a significant number of other countries, such as France, Germany, Australia and the US, have been relentlessly fighting against the so-called 'tampon tax'.

Laura Coryton, the initiator of the global *change.org* campaign relating to the tampon tax, describes the problem as follows: "[a]round the world, millions are being taxed for the 'luxury' of dealing with menstruation in the only socially acceptable way possible: by using sanitary products. Tampon tax needs to end. Period.".[1]

The tax treatment provoking women's reaction can be illustrated by means of the British 'tampon tax'. As frequently invoked by the opponents

---

1 www.change.org/m/end-the-sexist-and-illogical-tax-on-tampons-sanitary-pads-and-moon cups-period#about-movement [last accessed on 22 February 2018].

of the tax concerned, in the UK, women's sanitary protection products are subject to a 5% VAT and thereby treated as a 'non-essential luxury item'; whereas other products, such as foodstuff (including but not limited to edible cake decorations, marshmallow teacakes, pitta bread, kangaroo meat and crocodile meat), bingo, aircraft repair and maintenance, houseboat moorings and incontinence products are zero rated, i.e. deemed to be 'basic necessities' (or 'essential items').[2]

The tampon tax debate inevitably extended to the existing sex inequalities, especially with regard to parliamentary representation. It is undisputed that women's parliamentary representation has been traditionally low. Even if the seats held by women in national parliaments worldwide increased from 11.692 to 23.651 in the last decade,[3] a mere 23% of the available parliament seats are currently occupied by women.[4] It has been argued on several occasions that the presence of a tampon tax is one of the by-products of this lack of adequate representation. This view was also verbalized by Barack Obama, the former president of the US, who stated that:

> I have no idea why states would tax these [tampons] as luxury items. I suspect it's because men were making the laws when those taxes were passed. I think it's pretty sensible for women [. . .] to work to get those taxes removed.[5]

The core of the public debate on the tampon tax is best summarized by the speech of Stella Creasy (Labour MP[6]) made on 26 October 2015 in the House of Commons:

> Tampons and sanitary towels [. . .] have always been considered a luxury. That isn't by accident, that's by design of an **unequal society, in which the concerns of women are not treated as equally as the concerns of men**.

---

2 VAT rates applied in the UK are available on the website of the government on the following link www.gov.uk/guidance/rates-of-vat-on-different-goods-and-services [last accessed on 1 March 2018].
3 From 1997–2017.
4 Data collected by Inter-Parliamentary Union, available on the website of World Bank, on the following link: https://data.worldbank.org/indicator/SG.GEN.PARL.ZS [last accessed on 28 February 2018].
5 Interview of Barrack Obama conducted by Ingrid Nilsen available on the following link: www.youtube.com/watch?v=GYBGYFTCS9s [last accessed on 22 February 2018].
6 'MP' stands for 'Member of Parliament'.

Jaffa Cakes are zero rated, [. . .] but I do not consider them to be essential to my life. [. . .]

I recognise that razors are zero rated; judging by some of the members opposite, the opportunity to shave every day is for many of them a human right. [. . .]

Pitta bread is zero rated. What is the kebab, without a good pitta bread around it? It is a necessity.

It is when you start looking at what is described as **a necessity** and what is described as **a luxury** that you see the inequalities in this debate.[7]

B Underlying problem: consumption tax rates applied to women's sanitary protection products

The term 'tampon tax' refers to the consumption tax levied on women's sanitary protection products. To analyze whether the public reaction to the tampon tax is justified, this section concentrates on main characteristics of consumption tax systems (B.1 to B.4) and adequate classification of sanitary protection products within the systems concerned (B.5 to B.6).

Consumption taxes vary from country to country. Tampons, however, are generally submitted to tax by means of general (broad-based)[8] consumption taxes. For the purposes of the analysis conducted in this book, the reference will mainly be made to VAT, and in some cases to GST, the counterpart of VAT in some countries, such as Australia and Canada.

B.1 Consumption tax: the 'fairest' of them all?

Consumption has traditionally been considered as a fairer and more accurate measure of individual welfare than income. It is often argued that consumption is effectuated on a more voluntary basis when compared to earning income and that it demonstrates what a given person can afford to acquire in a given moment in a more reliable manner.[9] Consumption taxes levied on 'luxury items', such as alcohol and perfumes, may, *prima facie*, support this point of view. Taxes paid on such non-vital articles may be controlled, as Hamilton[10] stated, by individuals themselves: "[t]he rich can be extravagant, the poor can be frugal; and private oppression may always be

---

7 Emphasis added by the author. The video of the speech is available on the following link: www.huffingtonpost.co.uk/2015/10/27/stella-creasy-perfectly-sums-up-why-tampons-are-not-luxury-items_n_8399402.html [last accessed on 22 February 2018].
8 Consumption taxes levied on a number of goods and services.
9 See, for example, Vermeend, Ploeg and Timmer, p. 187.
10 Alexander Hamilton, one of the Founding Fathers of the US.

avoided by a judicious selection of objects proper for such impositions".[11] Low-income earners may avoid a heavy consumption tax burden simply by abstaining from buying luxury articles submitted to tax. When considered uniquely under this perspective, consumption taxes levied on luxury items may indeed be considered as fair and "hurtful to no man".[12]

Such an evaluation does not, however, take into consideration that consumption taxes are regressive, even when they are levied solely on luxury items. In fact, the higher the income of an individual becomes, the lower the percentage of his/her income spent to reimburse consumption taxes on luxuries is.[13] This is mainly due to the fact that the income of a person and his/her luxury consumption does not systematically increase in an equal manner. For instance, a person earning twice his/her income when compared to the last fiscal year does not necessarily buy twice as much tobacco, alcohol and other non-essential articles chosen for taxation.[14] His/her consumption of luxury items may even remain the same. Therefore, the extravagance of the rich and the frugality of the poor do not seem, *per se*, to create a complete fairness of consumption taxes on luxuries, which correspond to a much greater percentage of the income of the low-income earners in comparison to high-income earners.

The problems caused by the regressive character of consumption taxes are even more pronounced in case of consumption taxes levied on 'basic necessities'[15] or broad-based consumption taxes levied on a wide range of goods and services, combining luxury items and necessities, like VAT. Some goods and services are 'essential'; they must be purchased in order to sustain a dignified life, and in some cases merely for preserving life, regardless of the budget available. The most typical examples are basic foodstuff (like bread) and pharmaceutical products. Low-income earners cannot reasonably be expected to 'control' the consumption tax they pay on such items by abstaining from buying them.

The idea is often invoked that high-income earners spend more on basic necessities as well and thereby they contribute more in any case. Although this may hold true to a certain extent, it must be borne in mind that the basic necessities required for survival are almost equal for every human being. All consumption effectuated on top of that 'survival threshold' may

11 Hamilton quoted in Eisenstein, p. 17.
12 The early 17th-century Swedish chancellor, Axel Oxenstierna, stated that consumption taxes were "pleasing to God, hurtful to no man, and not provocative of rebellion". Quoted in Webber and Wildavsky, p. 272.
13 On this point, see, for example, Silverman, p. 70.
14 Silverman, p. 70.
15 Some basic necessities, like salt, were subject to tax throughout history, either due to their scarcity or for revenue collection purposes. Such taxes are not likely to exist in modern tax systems.

be considered as an extra. Without a shadow of a doubt, the consumption tax levied on goods and services necessary for survival corresponds to a much higher percentage of low-income earners' overall income than that of high-income earners' overall income.

As a matter of fact, the lower the income is, the heavier the consumption tax burden becomes. A low-income household barely making ends meet generally spends its income in its entirety to basic necessities. The cost incurred by the consumption tax is highly likely to force this income group to forgo some of the basic necessities they could have otherwise afforded. A mid-income level household is not likely to fall under the obligation to refrain from purchasing essential items due to the consumption tax. It may, however, have to abstain from buying other more non-essential items it could have otherwise afforded. Finally, consumption taxes do, generally, not cause any significant problems for high-income households.

B.2 Implementing intrasystem remedies for VAT's regressivity: an efficient strategy or a mere illusion of 'fairness'?

VAT has a standard rate that is applied to the majority of the goods and services subject to tax.[16] To address the regressivity issue, most countries opt for including in their VAT system some exceptions to this general rule. These exceptions are: (i) reduced rates, (ii) zero rate and (iii) exemptions.

Reduced rates consist of applying a lower rate than the standard rate to certain goods and services which are considered to be either 'essential' or significant for other purposes (such as encouragement of culture and sports). For instance, some of the goods and services that may be submitted to reduced rates by the EU Member States are foodstuffs, supply of water, pharmaceutical products, books, admission to cultural events and use of sporting facilities.[17] All EU countries, with the notable exception of Denmark, make use of reduced rates.[18]

The practices of zero rate and exemption are similar to a certain extent. Under both mechanisms, consumers do not officially pay a VAT on goods/ services concerned. The difference resides in the deductibility of the input

---

16 In the EU the standard rates vary between 17 (Luxembourg) and 27 (Hungary). The list of VAT rates used by EU Member States is available online on the following link: http://ec.europa.eu/taxation_customs/sites/taxation/files/resources/documents/taxation/vat/how_vat_works/rates/vat_rates_en.pdf [last accessed on 1 March 2018].

17 The list of supplies of goods and services that may be subject to reduced rates is provided in the Annex III of the Directive 2006/112.

18 The list of rates used by EU Member States is available online on the following link: http://ec.europa.eu/taxation_customs/sites/taxation/files/resources/documents/taxation/vat/how_vat_works/rates/vat_rates_en.pdf [last accessed on 1 March 2018].

VAT. While the zero rate system allows the supplier to credit the input VAT, the exemption mechanism does not. Accordingly, **zero rated** transactions are **free of VAT**, whereas **exempt** transactions may give rise to a **VAT charge** for the supplier. This additional cost incurred by the supplier is highly likely to be reflected in the prices it charges and to constitute, thereby, an 'invisible' (i.e. hidden) tax charge for consumers. Both zero rating and exemptions are commonly used strategies by countries to alleviate the VAT burden of low-income households. For instance, in the UK, some foodstuffs and equipment for disabled people are zero rated, and sponsored charitable events are tax exempt.[19]

Goods and services that are exempt and the ones submitted to a reduced or zero rate are determined freely by states. The states' discretion may, however, be subject to limitations. For instance, EU Member States are under the obligation to respect the provisions of the Directive 2006/112, which regulates the number of reduced rates that can be applied by Member States, goods and services that may be submitted to a reduced rate or to a zero rate, and goods and services that may be tax exempt. Traditionally, VAT laws do not fix general criteria that need to be fulfilled by a product or a service to qualify for a reduced/zero rate or exemption. They only contain exhaustive lists of supplies that benefit from such exceptions.

Two main reasons motivate countries to include exceptions into their VAT systems: satisfying "the deep, widespread feelings of the people as to what is fair"[20] and reducing regressivity. The first aim may certainly be reached by these strategies. Collecting a consumption tax on basic necessities is not a policy that can easily find public support, as demonstrated by the tampon tax debate. Reduced rates, zero rating and exemptions effectively allow the public mind to be eased. The second aim, however, cannot be reached by making modifications in the VAT system as per the dominant opinion on the issue.

The effects produced by multiple VAT rates are deemed to be quite limited. It is often argued that even though the poor may spend a large proportion of their income on the basic necessities, the rich are likely to spend more on such necessities in *absolute* terms.[21] Thereupon, most of the revenue forgone by either exempting the items concerned or taxing them at a reduced or zero rate effectively accrues to the rich and not to the poor.[22] To illustrate this point,

---

19 VAT rates applied in the UK are available on the website of the government on the following link www.gov.uk/guidance/rates-of-vat-on-different-goods-and-services [last accessed on 01 March 2018].
20 Schenk and Oldman, p. 74.
21 Keen, p. 224.
22 *Ibid.*

Keen gives the example of a study conducted by the OECD (in 2007) on the distributional impact of zero rating in Mexico. The study demonstrates that for each $100 forgone by zero-rating, less than $5 benefits the poorest 10% of the population, whereas more than $20 benefits the richest 10%.[23] Despite the fact that this example seems to support the dominant view, it must be underlined that, given the diminishing marginal utility of wealth, $5 to low-income budgets constitutes a much more significant contribution than $20 to high-income budgets. In other words, the zero rate put in place in Mexico seems to accrue more to the poorest 10% than to the richest 10% of the country in terms of economic impact. When the overall amount collected by means of VAT, which has the reputation of being a 'money machine',[24] is taken into consideration, it can be assumed that reduced rates and zero rates do generate a positive effect on low-income budgets.

This being stated, as per the prevalent view, even if such an impact may exist, it is revealed to be rather insignificant when compared to the effect that may be produced by means of other methods. First, income taxes are considered to be more efficient tools to enable the proper redistribution of income. Second, regarding the VAT system, it is considered that the focus should not be merely on the incidence of the tax but on the combined effect of the tax and how its revenue is spent.[25] Spending a part of the VAT proceeds to provide subsidies to low-income households (e.g. food stamps, subsidized rents etc.) and to increase public provision of goods and services (like basic health, education and infrastructure) can substantially reduce poverty.[26] A single-rate VAT is, thereby, justified: by making a rather small contribution, low-income households can benefit from a large variety of public services and subsidies, which are predominantly financed by means of the taxes paid by the rich. As put by the economist John Kenneth Galbraith, a uniform rate VAT has the merit of making public goods more abundant by making private goods more expensive.[27]

B.3 A single-rate VAT versus a multiple-rate VAT

According to the prevailing opinion on the matter, the 'good' VAT is a single-rate VAT with a comprehensive base, excluding only supplies that are too difficult to tax, such as financial services and insurance. This predominant opinion does not find its roots merely on the increased ability to

23 *Ibid*, pp. 224–225.
24 James, p. 25.
25 Schenk and Oldman, p. 9.
26 Keen, p. 228.
27 John Kenneth Galbraith quoted in Schenk and Oldman, p. 9.

provide more extensive public services and subsidies to low-income earners by means of VAT proceeds but in a number of other factors, which can be summarized as follows:[28]

1 A single-rate and broad-based VAT does not interfere, or interferes less than other taxes, with market decisions relating to patterns of consumption, production, distribution and saving (the so-called 'neutrality' of VAT). Multiple rates and extensive exemptions destroy neutrality and affect the patterns concerned.

2 A uniform standard rate decreases administration costs and makes compliance significantly effortless both for taxpayers and for tax administrations.

3 A single-rate system ensures legal certainty and simplicity by eliminating the problem of determining whether similar products should be subject to a standard, a reduced or a zero rate depending on their intrinsic characteristics. Multiple rates constitute a significant burden for tax administrations and courts, which are frequently forced to analyze features of different products to decide whether they qualify for a reduced/ zero rate or not. For instance, the Court of Appeal of the UK had to determine whether 'Pringles'[29] were made from potatoes.[30]

4 Countries applying a single standard rate generally adopt lower rates, which in turn decreases the overall consumption tax burden.

5 Despite the fact that in some sectors reduced VAT rates have been proven to be efficient,[31] overall experience shows that they rarely achieve their objective.[32] In fact, VAT cuts are seldom passed on to customers.

With regard to this last point, it is important to underline that the positive impact of lower VAT rates on the prices of goods and services cannot be excluded altogether. According to the final report of the study on reduced VAT applied to goods and services in the EU Member States,

> there is little doubt that permanently lowering the VAT rate on a particular good (or service) sooner or later will lead to a reduction in the price of the good more or less corresponding to the monetary equivalent of the lower VAT rate. If the VAT rate goes down by 10 percentage points on a good with a before tax price of €100, the price paid by the consumer will sooner or later drop by €10 for the vast majority of

---

28 Owens, Battiau and Charlet; Crawford, Keen and Smith, pp. 290–291; Boadway, pp. 51–73 and 134–135; James, pp. 20–27 and Schenk and Oldman, p. 28.
29 Pringles is an American brand of snacks.
30 *HMRC v Procter & Gamble UK* [2009] EWCA Civ 407.
31 Reduced VAT Study, p. 9 ff.
32 Owens, Battiau and Charlet.

products. In economics jargon, there will be a strong tendency towards full pass-through.[33]

Discussing whether a single-rate system is more efficient than a multiple-rate system or not does not fall within the scope of this book. As a matter of fact, the debate relating to the tampon tax exists in VAT systems that already provide for reduced rates and rather extensive lists of zero rates and exemptions. Although it can be argued that all exceptions to the standard rate should be kept at a minimum level for an efficient VAT system, in cases where a certain distinction is already being made between different consumption items, the fairness of the distinction concerned must be safeguarded. This implies that all the exceptions provided must include all items that share substantially similar characteristics.

B.4 Relation between reduced rates and price elasticity

Generally, the price of an item produces a reverse effect on the quantity of its demand, i.e. the higher the price the less in demand the good or the service. This effect can be more pronounced for some goods and services (high elasticity) and less pronounced for others (low elasticity). Then there are some 'inelastic' goods and services, which are continuously purchased regardless of their price. 'Essential' goods and services that constitute the 'basic necessities' of human beings are inelastic items.[34]

Inelastic behaviour forms a less mobile, more reliable and therefore a more efficient tax base. Luxury items are rather price-sensitive (elastic), whereas essential items are not, which makes the latter a more efficient tax base. The interference of a consumption tax levied on inelastic items with the market dynamics will be inconsequential, since a price increase is not likely to affect the purchase of the products/services concerned.

This being stated, the obligation to pay a consumption tax on an 'essential' item tends to create a feeling of 'unfairness' in the public eye, since a great part, if not the entirety, of low-income households' budgets is spent on such items. The lower the price of an essential item the richer the variety of other products that may be consumed by low-income households. For instance, the cheaper the foodstuff the more low-income earners dispose of available funds to purchase other goods, which may be considered more 'luxurious', like clothing items. Conversely, the higher the price of an essential item the more low-income households are compelled to limit their consumption of

33 Reduced VAT Study, p. 9.
34 While all essential items are inelastic, all inelastic items are not necessarily essential.

other products. In extreme cases, they may simply not afford all the 'essential' items and thereby be forced to choose some essential items over others.

B.5 The tampon: an 'inelastic' yet 'luxurious' item?

Sanitary protection products are the key to healthy menstrual periods. A woman's body is most vulnerable to infections during this time frame. Poor hygiene, due to lack of adequate products, causes the risk of infection to soar. The medical consequences of not having access to suitable sanitary products include skin rashes, urinary tract infection, genital infection, tubal obstructions, infertility and worsening of certain existent diseases.[35] Needless to say, these health problems may be further aggravated by non-adequate sterilization of the items used instead of sanitary protection products. For instance, trying to dry the sanitary protection in dark places (in order to avoid its exposure to other persons) enhances the growth of bacteria and microbes on the protection concerned.[36]

Lacking adequate sanitary protection products also largely prevents women from continuing their daily lives. World Bank statistics highlight that due to lack of sanitary protection products, girls can miss up to four days of school in every four-week period, i.e. 10% to 20% of their school days.[37] Similarly, women not having access to appropriate sanitary protection products have to abstain from going to work during their menstrual periods. For instance, 94% of the women who participated in the study conducted by WSSCC and UN Women in the Kedougou Region of Senegal (where sanitary protection products are not readily available to all women) indicated that they could not go to work during their periods.[38]

Although the idea of 'luxury' is vague and tends to vary from one year to another in the same country and from one country to another at the same time,[39] it seems quite straightforward that women's sanitary protection products are not luxurious but essential items. A woman who is under the obligation to use other items, like cloth, instead of sanitary protection products faces not only serious health problems but also an unpleasant odour that may, on its own, prevent her from leaving the house. The difficulties of sterilizing the item (most likely a piece of cloth) used as sanitary protection

---

35 Menstrual Hygiene Study, p. 56.
36 *Ibid.*
37 Hygiene Toolkit, Basic Principles/Inclusion & Participation/Gender Roles and Impact, available on the following link: www.wsp.org/Hygiene-Sanitation-Water-Toolkit/Basic Principles/GenderRoles.html [last accessed on 2 March 2018].
38 Menstrual Hygiene Study, p. 57.
39 Norman, p. 82.

is another burden, most commonly accompanied with the need to hide the item concerned. Women simply cannot pursue their regular lives in the absence of suitable sanitary protection products. Considering that menstrual periods occur, roughly, once a month, lack of such products constitutes a significant obstacle for women. Hence, it is undisputable that women's sanitary protection products are essential items.

Since sanitary protection products are essential, they are also 'inelastic'. Under normal circumstances, women will not be discouraged from purchasing sanitary protection products because of their price or the additional cost incurred by a consumption tax.

It is interesting to note that during the public debate relating to the tampon tax, women's sanitary protection products have often been compared with the so-called 'men's hygiene products', i.e. razors and shaving cream. The rationale behind this comparison is, to say the least, not comprehensible. It is evident that men who use regular soap over shaving cream or an electric shaver that does not require the use of a shaving cream do not suffer from any health problems or interruption of their routine activities. Men who go to a barber instead of shaving at home clearly do not encounter any life-changing problems, either. The fact that men's hygiene products were even mentioned in the tampon tax debate indicates that the obvious needs to be stated: the level of necessity of men's hygiene products and that of women's sanitary protection products are so far apart that the essential character of these two distinct types of products cannot reasonably be compared with each other.

B.6 Core of the problem: taxing sanitary protection products more heavily than other comparable items

The core of the problem resides in treating women's sanitary protection products as non-essential items and taxing them accordingly, i.e. at the standard rate. For instance, Annex III (3) of the Directive 2006/112 allows EU Member States to apply a reduced rate to "pharmaceutical products of a kind normally used for healthcare, prevention of illnesses and as treatment for medical and veterinary purposes, including products used for contraception and **sanitary protection**".[40] However, despite the availability of such an option, a great number of Member States do not opt for applying a reduced rate to sanitary protection products. For example, Finland applies the reduced rate of 10% to the items listed in Annex III (3), with the notable exception of products for contraception and sanitary protection, which are subject to the standard rate of 24%.[41] Similarly, Hungary applies a reduced

40 Emphasis added by the author.
41 VAT Compass, p. 668.

rate of 5% to traditional herbal medicine on the basis of the same regulation but subjects sanitary protection products to the standard rate of 27%.[42] The situation in the UK slightly differs from Finland and Hungary. Sanitary protection products are already subject to the reduced rate of 5%. What is being demanded by women is the zero rating of the products concerned, like foodstuff, children's clothing and books, which currently benefit from zero rate.

As a matter of fact, what is being required by women's organizations is quite straightforward and understandable: if some goods and services are considered to be 'essential' to human life and thereby subject to a reduced or zero rate, sanitary protection products should be one of these items. This is simply due to the fact that they are as essential as foodstuff for women's lives. They need to be as affordable as possible, and thereby subject to a VAT rate as low as possible, to allow a greater proportion of the population to purchase them.

C Impact of the tampon tax in numbers

While the 'unfairness' of the tampon tax is highly mediatized and widely discussed, its economic impact is much less debated. Despite this lack of interest, the economic consequences of the tax concerned is one of the most important elements that need to be taken into consideration while forming an informed opinion on the issue. For this reason, before analyzing the tampon tax further, its financial influence on the average women and on governments' budgets will be briefly and approximately laid out.

C.1 Impact on the average woman

In the research forming the basis of the congressional discussion for the US Tampon Safety and Research Act of 1997, it was established that 70% of the menstruating women in the US are opting for tampons out of all women's sanitary protection products.[43] Although it is not possible to establish with certainty which sanitary product is preferred over others (especially given the fact that women also tend to combine different products), for the sake of simplicity and given the frequency of its use, which may be presumed on the basis of the research conducted in the US, only tampons will be employed for the determination of the economic impact of the tampon tax on the average woman.

The approximate number of tampons that may be used by the average woman during her lifetime seems to vary between 9,600 and 11,400.[44] For

---

42 *Ibid*, p. 674.
43 US Congress Discussion, p. 2.
44 The US Congress Discussion indicates an approximate number of 11,400 (p. 2). Online research conducted by the author indicated that the approximate number seems to vary between 9,600 and 11,400.

the purposes of the calculations that will follow, it will be assumed that the number of tampons used by the average woman equals 10,500 (i.e. the average of 9,600 and 11,400).

Three countries will be used to measure the economic impact of the tampon tax, namely the UK,[45] Hungary and Australia (Table 6.1).

In the light of this brief analysis, it is possible to conclude that the economic impact of the tampon tax on the average woman is quite modest, even when the standard VAT/GST rate is applied to the products concerned.

Table 6.1

	UK	Hungary	Australia
Price of Tampax Regular[46]	£2.35[47]	€3.85[48]	$6.69[49]
Number of tampons included in one pack	18	32	20
Approximate number of packs needed in a lifetime[50]	583	328	525
Total cost of tampons in a lifetime[51]	£1,371	€1,263,28	$3,512,25
VAT/GST rate on women's sanitary products	5%	27%	10%
Total cost of VAT/GST incurred in a lifetime[52]	£66	€268.3	$319.3
Total cost of VAT/GST incurred per year[53]	£1.65	€6.7	$7.98

45 BBC provides for an online tampon tax calculator on its website. As per the calculator, a woman who menstruates for 40 years pays a tampon tax amounting to approximately £163.44 in her lifetime. The calculator is available on the following link: www.bbc.com/news/health-42013239 [last accessed on 1 March 2018].

46 The product chosen is the cheapest one available in all three countries in accordance with the information available online.

47 Tesco offers a pack of 20, whereas Sainbury's offers a pack of 18 tampons for this price. In fact, since August 2017, Tesco is applying a discount of 5% to all women's sanitary protection products to cover the cost of the VAT collected on these items itself. Prices of the Tampax products in the UK can be reached by means of the following link: https://tampax.co.uk/en-gb/buy-tampax-tampons/tampax-compak-tampons/tampax-compak-regular-applicator-tampons [last accessed on 25 February 2018].

48 According to the following website: www.expatistan.com/price/tampax/budapest/EUR [last accessed on 25 February 2018].

49 At Priceline Pharmacies, www.priceline.com.au/brand/tampax [last accessed on 25 February 2018]. It must be noted that the amount concerned is in Australian dollars and roughly equals US$5.18 [in February 2018].

50 Obtained by dividing the average number of tampons needed by a woman during her lifetime (i.e. 10,500) by the number of tampons contained in one pack of Tampax Compak Regular.

51 Obtained by multiplying the approximate number of packs needed during a lifetime with the price of one pack in the given country.

52 Obtained on the basis of the total cost of tampons in a lifetime and the VAT rate applied. For the sake of simplicity, it is considered that the VAT rate does not vary during the lifetime.

53 Assuming that the average women menstruates for 40 years.

C.2 Funds raised by governments

The economic impact of the tampon tax may be rather inconsequential on an individual level, but it is surely significant on a governmental level. Tampon taxes allowed to raise an annual amount of $20 million in California,[54] £15 million in the UK[55] and $36.5 million[56] in Canada.[57]

D Treating sanitary protection products as non-essential items cannot objectively be justified

The classification of women's sanitary protection products as non-essential items cannot be justified by any objective criterion. In cases where the applicable VAT/GST system makes a distinction between essential and non-essential products and subjects them to different tax rates, women's sanitary protection products must be considered as essential items and taxed accordingly. If more than one reduced rate and a zero rate are available, the rate applied to the products concerned should be equal to the rate applied to other basic necessities, like foodstuff.

Women's high sensibility on the issue mainly results from the sense of inequality deriving from the fact that women's sanitary products are being considered as non-essential items. When a tax is perceived to be unequal, a painful sensation is created in the part of the community subject to the tax concerned.[58] In the case of the tampon tax, there is no doubt that the tax concerned is unequal.

The facts that the demand for women's sanitary protection products is, in principle, inelastic and the economic impact of the tampon tax on individuals is rather limited should not cloud the importance of reducing the prices of sanitary protection products as much as possible. In fact, for low-income households, especially where most members of the family are women, sanitary protection can constitute a large chunk of

54 *Los Angeles Times*, Patrick McGreevy, "Tax-Free Tampons Measure Passes California Assembly", available online on the following link: www.latimes.com/politics/essential/la-pol-sac-essential-politics-california-tax-free-tampons-htmlstory.html [last accessed on 25 February 2018].
55 Sanitary Protection VAT Paper, p. 15.
56 Canadian dollars. The amount roughly equals US$28 million [in February 2018].
57 The GST on women's sanitary protection products was abolished in Canada as of July 2015. On this point see, for example, *Toronto Sun*, Postmedia Network, "Feds Scrap Tampon Tax", available online on the following link: www.torontosun.com/2015/05/28/feds-scrap-tampon-tax [last accessed on 25 February 2018].
58 On this point, see Norman, p. 53.

the family budget.[59] It is clear that in such cases all members of the family and not only women are affected, since the family may lack the necessary funds to purchase other basic necessities. The Trussell Trust reported that people using its foodbanks soared in 2014, with one of five working parents having to choose between paying an essential bill and buying food for the household.[60] Elevated prices of sanitary protection products add another layer to the dilemma: which essential item should be chosen over others?

Women who cannot afford tampons are not as rare as one might think. Some women opt for taking their contraceptive pills throughout the month in order to avoid "the cost of having a period".[61] In many US prisons, women must purchase their own sanitary products. With tampons costing approximately $5 a pack, many have to renounce the 'luxury'.[62] Under these circumstances, even a consumption tax that is deemed to be rather insignificant may produce an impact consequential enough to prevent women's access to the products concerned.

Given the difficulties encountered by a significant number of women on having access to sanitary protection products and the lack of an objective justification for the tampon tax, the public reaction on the issue is legitimate. As stated by Jyoti Sanghera, representative of the UN High Commissioner for Human Rights in Nepal, the "stigma around menstruation and menstrual hygiene is a violation of several human rights, most importantly the right to the human dignity".[63] It is clear that the stigma must be overcome, and governments have a key role in the fight against it.

---

59 Sanitary Protection VAT Paper, p. 11.
60 *Independent*, Natasha Preskey, "There Is Nothing Luxurious About My Periods, So Why Is the Government Taxing Tampons as If There Is?" available online on the following link: www.independent.co.uk/voices/comment/theres-nothing-luxurious-about-my-periods-so-why-is-the-government-taxing-tampons-as-if-there-is-10045629.html [last accessed on 25 February 2018].
61 *Ibid.*
62 *The Guardian*, Bridget Christie, "Bridget Christie: Feminine Products a Luxury? Hardly. At Least Jeremy Corbyn Understands", available online on the following link: www.theguardian.com/lifeandstyle/2015/oct/31/bridget-christie-corbyn-tampon-tax [last accessed on 25 February 2018].
63 www.ohchr.org/EN/NewsEvents/Pages/Everywomansrighttowatersanitationandhygiene.aspx [last accessed on 25 February 2018].

Bibliography

Books and academic articles

Boadway Robin, *From Optimal Tax Theory to Tax Policy, Retrospective and Pro-spective Views*, The MIT Press, 2012.

Crawford Ian, Keen Michael and Smith Stephen, Value Added Tax and Excises, in Mirrlees James (chair), Stuart Adam et al. (eds), *Dimensions of Tax Design, The Mirrlees Review*, Institute for Fiscal Studies, Oxford University Press, 2010.

Eisenstein Louis, *The Ideologies of Taxation, Rosenthal Lectures*, Ronald Press Company, 1961.

James Kathryn, *The Rise of the Value-Added Tax*, Cambridge Tax Law Series, Cambridge University Press, 2015.

Keen Michael, Targeting and Indirect Tax Design, in Clements Benedict, De Mooij Ruud, Gupta Sanjeev and Keen Michael (eds), *Inequality and Fiscal Policy*, International Monetary Fund, 2015.

Norman George Warde, *Taxation and the Promotion of Human Happiness*, D.P. O'Brien (ed), Edward Elgar Publishing, 2009.

Schenk Alan and Oldman Oliver, *Value Added Tax: A Comparative Approach in Theory and Practice*, Transnational Publishers, 2001.

Silverman Herbert Albert, *Taxation, Its Incidence and Effects*, Palgrave Macmillan, 1931.

Vermeend Willem, Ploeg Rick van der and Timmer Jan Willem, *Taxes and the Economy: A Survey on the Impact of Taxes on Growth, Employment, Investment, Consumption and the Environment*, Edward Elgar Publishing, 2008.

Webber Carolyn and Wildavsky Aaron, *A History of Taxation and Expenditure in the Western World*, Simon and Schuster, 1986.

Studies, reports, compilations and other similar documents

Congress Discussion for the USA Tampon Safety and Research Act 1997, *105th Congress, First Session, HR 2900 IH*, 7 November 1997, available online on the following link: www.congress.gov/105/bills/hr2900/BILLS-105hr2900ih. pdf [last accessed on 25 February 2018] (cited as USA Congress Discussion).

EU VAT Compass, 2017/2018, Annacondia Fabiola (ed), IBFD, 2017 (cited as VAT Compass).

Menstrual Hygiene Management: Behaviour and Practices in the Kedougou Region, Senegal, WSSCC and UN Women, 2015 (cited as Menstrual Hygiene Study).

Study on Reduced VAT Applied to Goods and Services in the Member States of the European Union, Copenhagen Economics, 2007 (cited as Reduced VAT Study).

Toolkit on Hygiene, Sanitation and Water in Schools, World Bank, available online on the following link: www.wsp.org/Hygiene-Sanitation-Water-Toolkit/index. html [last accessed on 02 March 2018] (cited as Hygiene Toolkit).

VAT on sanitary protection, prepared by Antony Seely, House of Commons Library, Briefing Paper, Number 01128, 15 December 2016 (cited as Sanitary Protection VAT Paper).

Other articles

Owens Jeffrey, Battiau Piet and Charlet Alain, *VAT's Next Half Century: Towards a Single Rate System?*, available online on the following link: http://oecdobserver. org/news/fullstory.php/aid/3509/VAT_s_next_half_century:_Towards_a_single-rate_system_.html [last accessed on 26 February 2018].

7   Government intervention

*"Have we not an equal interest with the men of this Nation in those liberties
and securities contained in the Petition of Right and other the good laws of
this Land? Are any of our lives, limbs, liberties or goods to be taken from us
more than from men, but by due process of Law?"*

—A women's petition written in 1649[1]

A Need for government intervention

The pink tax and tampon tax are not similar from a legal perspective: one
is a tax (tampon tax) and the other one is not (pink tax). They are, however,
extremely similar from an economic standpoint: they both give rise to a
compulsory and unrequited payment of an additional amount upon purchase
of supplies. More importantly, their target group is identical: females.

The relevant reasons that render a government intervention necessary
were already described separately for both practices in the previous chapters. This section demonstrates that government intervention is not only
necessary but also inevitable by means of three common characteristics
of the pink tax and tampon tax: (1) being untenable, (2) constituting 'bad
taxes' and (3) amounting to unlawful sex discrimination.

For the sake of simplicity and since it effectively is equivalent to a tax
on a purely economic level, the pink tax will be referred to as a 'tax' for the
purposes of this section.

A.1 The pink tax and tampon tax are untenable

"Taxes are what we pay for a civilized society".[2] Some taxes, however,
clearly do not fit with a civilized society. Quite the contrary: they contribute

---

1 The petition concerned was written in England, against martial law. Quoted in Wiesner, p. 245.
2 Oliver Wendell Holmes in *Compania General de Tabacos de Filipinas v Collector of Inter-
nal Revenue*, 275, U.S. 87, 100, 1927.

to the reinforcement of unfairness and inequality. Such taxes are abolished eventually, most commonly due to a persistent public effort aiming to pressurize politicians. Since most politicians initially opt for maintaining the *status quo*, the majority of these 'legal battles' last at least a decade. The arguments advanced by some politicians to support the tax concerned tend to be even more disturbing than the tax itself.

For instance, the newspaper stamp duty (also referred to as 'tax on knowledge'), which existed between 1712 and 1855 in Great Britain, caused affordable newspapers that could be bought by the middle class to vanish, along with the possibility of a great part of the population to read a newspaper.[3] Nonetheless, conservative politicians were satisfied with that result since the tax on knowledge "placed newspapers under the control of respectable men, who for their own sakes, would conduct them in a more respectable manner than was likely to be the result of a pauper management".[4]

Similarly, the window tax, which existed in England between 1695 and 1851, forced people who could not afford the tax to block every possible window, which in turn resulted in houses becoming unbearably malodorous, polluted and in some cases covered with mould.[5] Fiscal considerations caused the tax to be maintained, even long after the serious public health hazard generated by it had become apparent.[6] In fact, each time the issue of health problems provoked by the window tax was raised, politicians merely made sarcastic comments. For instance, when Dr. Southwood Smith, from the Metropolitan Improvement Society, visited Henry Goulburn, the chancellor at the time, in 1844 to draw his attention to severe health consequences of the window tax, the chancellor expressed 'his entire disbelief' in the observations made. Scrofula (a disease with glandular swellings, which was allegedly caused by poor ventilation), the chancellor indicated, existed in the rural cottages of the poor, who were exempt from the window tax.[7] On another occasion, the chancellor also stated that if the opponents could propose a hole that would admit air but not light, it would not be chargeable as a window.[8]

Today, a tax on knowledge or on daylight appears to be inconceivable and necessarily belonging to ancient times. Yet the pink tax and tampon tax are no different than a window tax or a tax on knowledge, in their essence. Sanitary protection products are qualified as 'non-essential' items for VAT/

---

3 Oats and Sadler, pp. 292–293.
4 *Ibid*, p. 292.
5 Stebbings, p. 56.
6 *Ibid*, p. 43.
7 *Ibid*, p. 63.
8 *Ibid*.

GST purposes, and the sheer fact of being women gives rise to an additional amount being charged on a great variety of services and products available on the market. Both taxes seem to be relics of ancient times, but they are currently being collected in our modern societies.

Not even one reasonable criterion that may justify gender-based pricing or the tampon tax exists. Nonetheless, these taxes are still being levied. The rationale behind the lack of government intervention seems to be highly similar to the factors behind the long-time refusal of amending or abolishing the window tax.

First, governments seem to be concerned about the political signals that a 'coerced' zero (or reduced) rating and a set of limitations imposed on private companies' pricing policies would send. For the purposes of the window tax, the government was concerned about the influence the repeal of a national tax may have on the power to levy taxes, which constituted a potent characteristic of sovereignty and one of the most important functions of a government.[9] For the purposes of the tampon tax, it has been argued that if zero (or reduced) rating of sanitary protection products is granted, the debate may extend to other products and/or services that are submitted to VAT, which would produce an undesirable result, since to be efficient VAT should be as broadly based as possible.[10] Concerning the pink tax, the main obstacle is the reluctance to interfere with the free market economy.[11] Governments aim for safeguarding the economic efficiency as much as possible and seem to be preoccupied with the reaction that may be caused by such an interference.[12]

Second, the tampon tax, just as the window tax,[13] does produce a gain for governments, however modest it may be when compared to revenues raised by means of other taxes. This does not hold true for the pink tax, although it is possible to state that governments indirectly benefit from the revenues raised by private entities levying the pink tax.

Last but not least, vested interests in parliaments also play their part. For the window tax, some members of the Parliament were simply indifferent to the problems caused by the tax, and this apathy hindered the repeal of the tax.[14] On the other hand, some other members, who were property owners,

---

9 *Ibid*, p. 66.
10 On this point, see, for example, Sanitary Protection VAT Paper, p. 9.
11 On this issue, see, for example, Harvard Law Review, p. 1843.
12 For more details on this issue, see Chapter IV, Section F, titled "To perpetuate or to end, that is the question".
13 Stebbings, p. 67.
14 *Ibid*, p. 68.

had a direct interest in not abolishing the window tax.[15] Regarding gender-based pricing and the tampon tax, the main problem seems to be the apathy of most parliament members. As already mentioned,[16] parliaments are still heavily dominated by men, who may not be as preoccupied as women on these issues. This indifference may be illustrated by the statements made by Christian Eckert, the French state secretary for the budget at the time, during the vote conducted for an amendment to classify sanitary towels and tampons as essential products and thereby to reduce the applicable VAT rate from 20% to 5.5%. Eckert argued that the rate reduction concerned would be unfair to men "paying the full rate on shaving cream".[17] The state secretary also compared women's sanitary protection products to activities conducted in leisure parks by indicating that the government has also faced calls for reducing the VAT rate on activities such as leisure parks and grottos, but they had to reject them as well due to the public debt of €2.105 billion.[18]

A.2 The pink tax and tampon tax are 'bad taxes'

Quite interestingly, "[t]axes have often been the fuse that ignites the powder keg of human discontent",[19] and many of the great events in history, including most revolutions, have been rooted in taxation.[20] Bad taxes generally backfire, even if historically it takes a few decades or in some cases a generation for a backlash against bad taxation to bear fruit.[21] A 'bad tax' can be defined as any tax that people do not want and will not support.[22] People are the sole arbiter on the diagnosis of a bad tax; an expert opinion on the issue is not necessary.[23]

As can be observed by the great number of campaigns that were initiated on *change.org*, by the statements made by a number of women's rights organizations and politicians and simply by the overall public reaction, the pink tax and tampon tax are considered to be 'bad taxes'. These taxes have been around for more than a few decades. The earliest gender-pricing

15 *Ibid.*
16 In Chapter VI, Section A, titled "Public perception: 'Crocodile meat is considered to be an essential product, whereas tampons are deemed to be luxury items'".
17 *The Times*, Adam Sage, "French Women See Red over Tampon Tax", available on the following link: www.thetimes.co.uk/tto/news/world/europe/article4591377.ece [last accessed on 22 February 2018].
18 *Ibid.*
19 Adams, p. 448.
20 *Ibid.*
21 *Ibid*, p. 379.
22 *Ibid*, p. 382.
23 *Ibid.*

studies that could be found by the author date back to the 1990s, which implies that the problem existed before that period. The implementation of the VAT dates back approximately to the 1970s,[24] which indicates that the tampon tax has been levied for approximately 40 years. The public reaction to these taxes is not recent; it began in the early 2000s. Nevertheless, the opposition has become more intense and persistent in the last four years. It seems that 'the powder keg' of the discontent on pink and tampon taxes' fuse has been ignited and is ready to explode, unless governments decide to intervene. In the meantime, some individual enterprises are beginning to take action against these taxes due to public pressure. As already mentioned, a chief example is Tesco, who taken measures to alleviate the effects of both the pink tax and the tampon tax.

A.3 The pink tax and tampon tax amount to unlawful sex discrimination

To demonstrate that the pink tax and tampon tax are discriminatory, first the principle of non-discrimination is briefly described (1). Second, non-discrimination clauses that may be applied to the pink tax and tampon tax are mentioned (2). Third, sex discrimination is examined from a tax law perspective (3). Finally, both taxes are analyzed in the light of the principle of non-discrimination (4).

A.3.1 Principle of non-discrimination

Discrimination can be broadly defined as treating an individual less favourably due to his/her belonging to a certain group so as to deprive him/her of some opportunities which would have been available to him/her in the ordinary course of events.[25] The principle of non-discrimination, which aims to prevent such less favourable treatment, derives from the principle of equality but is not an exact equivalent of the latter.[26] One of the main differences between the two principles resides in the significance of group belonging for discrimination purposes. An individual is discriminated against when he/she is treated less favourably for being a part of a group.[27] These groups are commonly referred to as 'discrimination grounds'.

---

24 Thuronyi, p. 305.
25 The principle of non-discrimination may apply to legal entities and include other aspects than those that are described in this subsection. This book mentions only the aspects relevant for the purposes of the analysis that is being conducted.
26 For more information on this point, see, for instance, Schiek, Waddington and Bell, pp. 69–70.
27 Schiek, Waddington, Bell, p. 70.

Non-discrimination clauses generally contain a list of prohibited grounds, which may either be a closed list (i.e. exhaustive list) or an open-ended list (i.e. a list of examples). While the prohibited grounds may vary to a certain degree, some grounds are systematically contained in every non-discrimination clause. These include, but are not limited to, **sex**, race and religion (the so-called 'suspect grounds'). Since these grounds can rarely be considered as constituting a reasonable base for unequal treatment, their existence immediately raises a suspicion of unreasonableness and prejudice.[28] Justifying a distinction based on a suspect ground necessitates more weighty reasons when compared to other non-suspect grounds.

The discrimination ground that must be analyzed in detail for the purposes of the pink tax and tampon tax is sex, and not gender. The analysis conducted throughout this book has clearly established that both taxes target all females, regardless of their gender.

A.3.2 Definition of sex discrimination

Sex discrimination may be defined as any distinction, exclusion or restriction made on the basis of sex which is not reasonably and objectively justified as a proportionate means to achieve a legitimate aim and which has the effect or purpose of impairing or nullifying the exercise or enjoyment of internationally protected human rights, fundamental freedoms in the political, economic, social, cultural or any other field, and rights under national laws.

Discrimination may take two forms: direct and indirect. Direct sex discrimination is a different treatment explicitly based on grounds of sex differences, whereas indirect sex discrimination occurs "when a law, policy, programme or practice appears to be neutral as it relates to men and women but has a discriminatory effect in practice on women"[29] or men.

A.3.3 Prohibition of sex discrimination in legal systems

Most constitutions provide for a specific clause relating to the equality between men and women and/or a non-discrimination clause enumerating a number of prohibited grounds,[30] which generally include sex. Accordingly, in most countries, the constitution forms a source that allows sex discrimination to be

---

28 Gerards, p. 79.
29 Byrnes, p. 65.
30 See, for example, article 7 (1) and (2) of the Austrian Constitution and article 8 (2) and (3) of the Swiss Constitution. Available on the UN Women's Global Gender Equality Constitutional Database, http://constitutions.unwomen.org/en/search?keywords=austria&provisioncategory=b21e8a4f9df246429cf4e8746437e5ac [last accessed on 4 March 2018].

counteracted. This being stated, constitutional protection against discrimination is not absolutely universal. The states without any national obligations must, however, still ensure the prohibition of sex discrimination, since the prohibition concerned is contained in a number of international treaties. It may even be argued that prohibition of sex discrimination has become a part of customary law and a general principle of law. On this point, Cassel and Guzman state that

> [o]utside the Islamic world, [. . .] the case for a customary international law rule against [sex] discrimination, based on its repeated expression in treaties ratified and declarations adopted by the overwhelming majority of non-Islamic states, is now solid.[31]

The authors further state that "the legal acceptance by states of the principle that [sex] discrimination is impermissible is now so nearly universal as to qualify as a 'general principle of law'".[32]

While a number of international treaties expressly prohibit sex discrimination, the most far-reaching one is the CEDAW, elaborated by the UN, adopted in 1979 and ratified by 189 states. Women's equal participation in economic and social life is one of the fundamental freedoms that falls within the scope of application of the Convention. Equal participation in economic life is to be interpreted broadly and extends to tax matters. Equal participation to social life entails equal access to all services intended to be used by the general public.[33]

The protection offered by the CEDAW does not only cover discrimination due to an act or legislation of a state. It also extends to prevention and punishment of unlawful sex discrimination inflicted by private persons. As per article 2 (e) of the CEDAW, states parties are under the obligation to undertake all appropriate measures to eliminate discrimination against women by any person, organization or enterprise. Action taken against non-state actors, such as private individuals and corporations, constitutes an important component of protection against discrimination. States parties may not justify their failure to take action in these matters

> simply by averring powerlessness, or by explaining **inaction** through **predominant market or political forces**, such as those **inherent in the private sector**, private organizations, or political parties. States

---

31 Cassel and Guzman, p. 293. It is to be noted that Cassel and Guzman use the terms 'sex' and 'gender' interchangeably to differentiate men and women. The term 'gender discrimination' they originally used was converted to 'sex discrimination' by the author, since they are, in fact, referring to 'sex discrimination' as per the terminology adopted in this book.
32 *Ibid*, p. 295.
33 Article 13 of the CEDAW. For more information on this issue, see, for example, Rudolf.

parties are reminded that article 2 of the Convention, which needs to be read in conjunction with all other articles, imposes accountability on the State party for action by these actors.[34]

It is important to underline that the CEDAW follows an asymmetrical approach, i.e. it aims to protect women and not men. Some national or regional laws may be following a symmetrical approach, i.e. protecting both sexes in an equal manner. For instance, the European Directives generally opt for a symmetrical approach. In such cases, states may abstain from following the asymmetrical approach of the CEDAW for not infringing the provisions of other applicable laws and regulations.[35] For the purposes of the analysis conducted in this book, however, this issue is not relevant. Cessation of the pink tax and tampon tax through government intervention cannot possibly interfere with the rights or the interests of men in any manner.

A.3.4 Sex discrimination by means of consumption taxes

Explicit bias (equivalent of 'direct sex discrimination') can, as a general rule, not be found in consumption taxes,[36] since the tax liability of such taxes is established with respect to the purchase or production of a commodity.[37] This being stated, it is "possible to introduce such bias by establishing a tax based on the purchase of a commodity only when a woman (or man) buys it".[38] To the extent known by the author, this possibility has not been entertained so far.

This does not signify that consumption taxes are always sex neutral. They may give rise to implicit bias (equivalent of 'indirect sex discrimination'). Stotsky argues that indirect discrimination may result from differential consumption patterns of men and women or may be inherent to a decision made within the organizational structure of the tax itself.[39]

Differential consumption patterns of men and women may cause one sex to purchase more often the goods and/or services that are taxed at a lower rate. Although an implicit bias may occur in such cases, its existence

---

34 Emphasis added by the author. General recommendation No. 25, on article 4, paragraph 1, of the Convention on the Elimination of All Forms of Discrimination against Women, on temporary special measures, para 29.
35 Gerards, pp. 101–103.
36 As described in Chapters V and VI, the pink tax acts as and the tampon tax is a consumption tax.
37 Stotsky, p. 12.
38 *Ibid.*
39 *Ibid*, p. 13.

is difficult to establish in practice.[40] For the purposes of VAT/GST, a bias within the organizational structure of the tax itself can result from the lists of goods and services that may benefit from a reduced rate or zero rate.[41] To the extent where the lists concerned are established in a non-discriminating manner, existence of an implicit bias should, in principle, not be admitted. This is due to the fact that once the distinction is made in a correct and fair manner, inequality in tax incidence between those who consume luxury goods that attract higher rates and those who consume basic necessities that attract less tax cannot in itself be considered as amounting to indirect discrimination.[42] Nevertheless, an implicit bias should be deemed to exist in cases where a product/service most commonly used by one sex is taxed at a higher rate on purpose.

A.3.5 Analysis of the pink tax and tampon tax

The pink tax is the practice of over-pricing goods and services manufactured for/rendered to women. It has been established earlier[43] that this overpricing is oftentimes exclusively due to sex. Since women are expressly targeted by this practice on the basis of their sex, pink tax should be qualified as a case of **direct sex discrimination.**

By opting to submit women's sanitary protection products to the standard rate of VAT/GST or to a reduced rate, while other basic necessities are subject to a reduced rate or to zero rate, governments produce **an implicit bias** inherent to the organizational structure of the tax. As essential items, women's sanitary protection products must be submitted to the rate made available to other basic life necessities. Submitting sanitary protection products exclusively used by women to higher tax rates suggests that one sex (female) is being taxed at a higher rate on purpose.

It may be argued that since men do not have an equivalently essential product,[44] discrimination cannot occur. Such an approach is erroneous, as the relevant criterion to establish the presence of an implicit bias is the fact that one product or service that is typically used by one sex is being subject to a higher tax rate without any reasonable and objective ground. As already examined,[45] submitting products essential for women's health to a higher

---

40 *Ibid.*
41 *Ibid.*
42 Grown, p. 16.
43 See Chapter IV, titled "The 'pink tax' phenomenon".
44 Shaving creams and razors cannot be considered as life necessities, as developed in Chapter VI, Subsection B.5., titled "The tampon: an 'inelastic' yet 'luxurious' item?".
45 In Chapter VI, titled "Legal analysis of the 'tampon tax'".

rate than other basic necessities, like foodstuff, cannot be justified by any reasonable and objective ground.

It can therefore safely be stated that both the pink tax and the tampon tax constitute discriminatory practices that violate the applicable laws.

B Means of government intervention

It has been demonstrated that both the pink tax and the tampon tax need to be abolished from a socioeconomic point of view. It has also been established that these two practices are discriminatory and thereby violate the applicable laws and regulations. Inaction equalling action, governments choosing not to intervene are, in fact, endorsing and perpetuating these unlawful practices. By doing so, they are infringing their obligations deriving from international treaties, like the CEDAW,[46] along with the rights of women, which are universally recognized and considered as general principles of law.

The pink tax and tampon tax are highly different practices; so are the possible means of government intervention to abolish them.

B.1 Government intervention in the pink tax

An efficient way to abolish the pink tax would be the enactment of laws and/or regulations prohibiting gender-based pricing. The necessary level of regulation on the matter may be demonstrated by the example of the Gender Tax[47] Repeal Act of the State of California.[48] The Gender Tax Repeal Act, enacted in 1995, prohibited all discrimination "with respect to the price charged for services of similar or like kind against a person because of the person's gender".[49] The Act specified that nothing in it "prohibits price differences based specifically upon the amount of time, difficulty, or cost of providing the services".[50]

The Gender Tax Repeal Act constitutes an important milestone in the fight against the pink tax. This being stated, the impact of the Act is restrained due to two main factors: (i) its scope is limited to services and (ii) it specifically exempts from its scope differential pricing based on the amount

---

46 Regarding EU Member States, it may be argued that the practice of the pink tax violates the Council Directive 2004/113/EC of 13 December 2004 implementing the principle of equal treatment between men and women in the access to and supply of goods and services.
47 'Gender tax' refers to the 'pink tax' as per the qualification adopted in this book.
48 Assembly Bill No. 1088, Civil rights: Gender discrimination, State of California, 1995.
49 Section 1, 51.6 (b) of the Gender Tax Repeal Act.
50 Section 1, 51.6 (c) of the Gender Tax Repeal Act.

of time, difficulty or cost of providing the services. It is clear that the individual women (or men) who require burdensome services should be charged accordingly.[51] Nonetheless, women, as a group, should not be charged at a flat premium on the basis of a false presumption that they all require onerous services simply as a direct consequence of their sex.[52] By excluding from its scope differential pricing that may be justified on the basis of the pre-determined factors, the Gender Tax Repeal Act ultimately provides 'only feeble protection' against sex discrimination.[53] Service providers can systematically succeed in shielding themselves from liability by claiming that the higher prices reflect the greater burden associated with providing services to women.[54]

The proposed 2016 amendment of the Gender Tax Repeal Act,[55] which finally was not adopted, would have extended the scope of the Act to products. The Amendment provided that no price differentiation based on gender should be established with regard to goods of "a substantially similar or like kind".[56] The proposed amendment defined the goods of a substantially similar or like kind on the basis of the following criteria: (i) share the same brand; (ii) share the same functional components and (iii) share 90% of the same materials or ingredients.[57] The Amendment expressly specified that goods did not include foodstuff.[58]

An act or similar instrument, as allowed under the applicable law of a given country, akin to the Gender Tax Repeal Act may indeed eliminate the pink tax. It is, however, clear that the scope of the instrument should cover both products and services. Concerning services, the instrument should hold service providers liable to adopt transparent pricing policies and to charge additional costs exclusively on the basis of objective criteria, such as duration of the service and a specific material used to render the service. All pre-established prices based on sex must be explicitly prohibited. For the purposes of substantially similar or like kind goods, price disparities established on the basis of the targeted consumer group's sex should be proscribed. The criteria used in the proposed amendment of the Gender Tax Repeal Act are appropriate to determine goods that are substantially similar. The scope of the term 'goods' should not extend to goods that are clearly

---

51 Harvard Law Review, p. 1844.
52 *Ibid.*
53 *Ibid*, p. 1839.
54 *Ibid.*
55 SB–899, Gender discrimination: pricing, 2015–2016.
56 Section 1, 51.6 (b) (2) of the Amendment.
57 Section 1, 51.6 (e) (1) of the Amendment.
58 Section 1, 51.6 (e) (2) of the Amendment.

not targeted at a particular sex, such as foodstuff. Such goods should, however, be exhaustively enumerated in the instrument so as not to give rise to uncertainties in practice.

The designation of the legal instrument concerned is almost as important as its contents. An appropriate title would be 'Sex-Based Pricing Repeal Act', for the reasons enumerated in the previous chapters.[59] Should the mention of the term tax be deemed essential, the term 'Women's Products and Services Tax' (WPST) would be more suitable than 'Gender Tax' or 'Sex Tax'. This being stated, since the pink tax is not a tax in the legal sense, such a term may cause confusion.

B.2 *Government intervention in the tampon tax*

The tampon tax constitutes a government-induced implicit bias which is inherent to the organizational structure of the VAT/GST itself. Accordingly, government intervention in the tampon tax may merely consist of subjecting women's sanitary protection products to the same rate as other basic life necessities, as it was previously done in Canada and – at least to a great extent – in the UK. Since the lists of goods and services that are exempt or benefit from a reduced/zero rate are determined freely by the countries, proceeding to such a modification is not burdensome, at least for most countries.

The UK government had to engage in a lengthy 'legal battle' to zero rate women's sanitary products due to the applicable EU legislation on the matter, which prevents Member States from introducing a new zero rate. Only zero rates that had already been in place on 1 January 1991 (subject to conditions set forth in Title VIII, Chapter 4 of the Directive 2006/112) and those that benefit from an express derogation are allowed to be applied. For instance, sanitary protection products are zero rated in Ireland, since they were already zero rated prior to 1 January 1991.

Despite this legal obstacle, the UK government has put a significant effort in the fight against the tampon tax. The UK's firm approach and persistent struggle paved the way for the European Commission's legislative proposal, published in January 2018, to introduce more flexibility for Member States to modify the VAT rates they apply to different supplies.[60] The proposed system provides for, among others, application of a third reduced rate[61] of between 0%

---

59 See Chapter II ("Gender versus sex") and Chapter III, Subsection B.2 ("From confusion to clarity: a specific term for each different concept").
60 The proposal is available on the following link: https://ec.europa.eu/taxation_customs/sites/taxation/files/18012018_proposal_vat_rates_en.pdf [last accessed on 25 February 2018].
61 Currently, as per articles 98 and 99 of the Directive 2006/112, Member States may apply either one or two reduced rates. The reduced rates cannot be less than 5%.

and 5%, abolition of the current list of goods and services to which reduced rates can be applied[62] and its replacement by a list of products to which the standard rate of minimum 15% must always be applied. It must be underlined that the legal obstacles, like the one faced by the UK, remain rare in practice.

A second manner of intervention would be to tax sanitary protection products at the standard or reduced rate and to provide public subsidies or services to women in need. Such a tax policy would be reasonable, since the financial burden provoked by the tampon tax on an individual basis is quite limited (less than $10 per year) but the funds that can be collected by governments are substantial (approximately $20 million). The tampon tax can provide governments with necessary funds to supply free sanitary protection products to all women who cannot afford them, the most typical example being the women in prison. It may also enable governments to assist women's rights organizations and similar associations that support women in need. This specific allocation of funds may 'justify' the tampon tax, not from a purely legal point of view but from a social welfare perspective. The UK already put in place such a system. Since November 2015, the VAT receipts deriving from sanitary protection products are granted to women's charities.[63] This allocation of funds is, however, only temporary and will continue until zero rate can effectively be applied.[64]

Bibliography

Books and academic articles

Adams Charles, *For Good and Evil: The Impact of Taxes on the Course of Civilization*, Madison Books, 2000.

Byrnes Andrew, Article 1, in Freeman Marsha A., Chinkin Christine and Rudolf Beate (eds), *The UN Convention on the Elimination of All Forms of Discrimination Against Women, A Commentary*, Oxford University Press, 2012.

Cassel Douglass and Guzman Jill, The Law and Reality of Discrimination Against Women, in Askin D. Kelly and Koenig Dorean M. (eds), *Women and International Human Rights Law*, Volume 1, Transnational Publishers, 1999.

Gerards Janneke, Discrimination Grounds, in Schiek Dagmar, Waddington Lisa and Bell Mark (eds), *Cases, Materials and Text on National, Supranational and International Non-Discrimination Law*, Ius Commune Casebooks for the Common Law of Europe, Hart Publishing, 2007.

Grown Caren, Taxation and Gender Equality, A Conceptual Framework, in Grown Caren and Valodia Imraan (eds), *Taxation and Gender Equity*, Routledge, 2010.

---

62 Annex III of the Directive 2006/112.
63 Sanitary Protection VAT Paper, p. 15.
64 *Ibid*, p. 17ff.

Oats Lynne/Sadler Pauline, The Abolition of the Taxes on Knowledge, in Tiley John (ed), *Studies in the History of Tax Law*, Volume 2, Hart Publishing, 2007.

Rudolf Beate, Article 13, in Freeman Marsha A., Chinkin Christine and Rudolf Beate (eds), *The UN Convention on the Elimination of all Forms of Discrimination Against Women, A Commentary*, Oxford University Press, 2012.

Schiek Dagmar, Waddington Lisa and Bell Mark, Introductory Chapter, A Comparative Perspective on Non-Discrimination Law, in Schiek Dagmar, Waddington Lisa and Bell Mark (eds), *Cases, Materials and Text on National, Supranational and International Non-Discrimination Law*, Ius Commune Casebooks for the Common Law of Europe, Hart Publishing, 2007.

Stebbings Chantal, Public Health Imperatives and Taxation Policy: The Window Tax as an Early Paradigm in English Law, in Tiley John (ed), *Studies in the History of Tax Law*, Volume 5, Hart Publishing, 2012.

Stotsky Janet G., *Gender Bias in Tax Systems*, IMF Working Paper, International Monetary Fund, Fiscal Affairs Department, 1996.

Thuronyi Victor, *Comparative Tax Law*, Kluwer Law International, 2003.

Wiesner Merry E., *Women and Gender in Early Modern Europe*, New Approaches to European History, Cambridge University Press, 1993.

Studies, reports and reviews

VAT on sanitary protection, prepared by Antony Seely, House of Commons Library, Briefing Paper, Number 01128, 15 December 2016 (cited as Sanitary Protection VAT Paper).

109 *Harvard Law Review*, 1995–1996, pp. 1839–1844 (cited as Harvard Law Review).

8 Conclusion

"A society can best be evaluated by examining who is taxed, what is taxed, and how taxes are assessed, collected and spent."[1] In Ancient Greece, where any type of direct taxation was considered to have demeaning overtones, the Athenians levied a monthly direct tax from foreigners, i.e. anyone who did not have both an Athenian mother and father, to humiliate them ('poll tax').[2] In the 18th and 19th centuries, slaves, who were assimilated to commodities, were submitted to tax in accordance with their characteristics. Import duties on slaves 'fresh from Africa' were lower than the ones levied on slaves coming from Caribbean islands, where slave revolts were frequent, to discourage the 'import' of the latter ('slave taxes').[3] Some other taxes levied during the same centuries deprived the middle class from having access to newspapers ('tax on knowledge') and the poor from having access to daylight and air ('window tax'). In the 21st century, men and women pay different amounts to purchase substantially similar products and services. The former pay less, the latter pay more ('pink tax'). Moreover, for consumption tax purposes, women's sanitary protection products are usually not considered as basic life necessities, whereas herbal medicines and admission to circuses are ('tampon tax').
  "History repeats itself, first as tragedy, second as farce".[4]

Bibliography

Adams Charles, *For Good and Evil: The Impact of Taxes on the Course of Civilization*, Madison Books, 2000.
Outterson Kevin, Slave Taxes, in Tiley John (ed), *Studies in the History of Tax Law*, Volume 1, Hart Publishing, 2004.

1 Adams, p. 448.
2 *Ibid*, p. 54.
3 Outterson, p. 271.
4 Karl Marx.

Index

androgynous 6

bad tax 78
basic (life) necessity 43, 49, 59–63,
  66–69, 71–72, 83–84, 86, 88
bounded rationality 17, 47
broad-based consumption tax *see*
  general consumption tax

cashews 18, 21
consumption 15–19, 60–62
consumption tax 43–44, 54, 60–62, 63,
  65, 66, 68, 72, 82

direct sex discrimination 80, 82, 83
discrimination (discriminatory) 43, 79,
  80, 81, 84
discrimination ground 79–80
doing gender 5, 28, 33–34

elasticity (elastic behaviour, elastic
  demand) 48, 49, 66
essential item *see* basic (life) necessity
exemption (VAT/GST) 62–66, 86
explicit bias 82

female 5–6
feminine (femininity) 5–6, 7–10, 21, 32
free market 16–17, 36–37, 52, 77
fully hidden tax 45–46, 54–55

gender 3–6, 28, 29, 80
gender-based pricing (gender-
  pricing) 23, 24–35, 50, 56, 77,
  78–79, 84

gendered colour 8
gendered products 31–33, 35
gender-neutral colour 8
gender socialization 28–30
gender stereotypes 27–31
gender tax 11–13, 84, 86
gender wage gap 1
general consumption tax 43, 60
Georgette Sand 10
GIRLTALKHQ 37, 55
GST 43, 60, 70–72, 77, 83, 86

hidden tax 44–50, 54–55, 63
hyper-rationality 15, 16

implicit bias 82–83, 86
indirect sex discrimination 80, 82, 83
inelasticity (inelastic behaviour,
  inelastic demand) 49, 54, 66–68, 71
input VAT 45, 63

luxury items (luxury goods) 49, 54,
  58–61, 66–68, 71–72, 77, 83

male 5–6
market 15, 16–17, 36
market maven 16
Marshmallow Test 22–23
masculine 5–6
men's hygiene products 68
multiple rate (VAT/GST) 63, 64–66

necessity (basic life) *see* basic (life)
  necessity
neoclassical school of economics 16–17

non-discrimination 79–80
non-essential goods (items) *see* luxury
  items

partially hidden tax 45–46
pink 7–10
pink tax 7–14, 15–38, 50–56, 75–79,
  80, 82, 83–86, 88
poll tax 88
principle of non-discrimination *see*
  non-discrimination
prohibited ground *see* discrimination
  ground

reduced rate (VAT/GST) 43, 62–66,
  68–69, 77, 83, 86–87
regressivity (of a tax) 61, 62–66

sanitary protection products 11–12, 13,
  58–60, 67–72, 76–77, 83, 86–87,
  88; *see also* tampon
Schrödinger's cat 40, 55–56
selective consumption tax 43, 53–54
self-control 15, 17–18, 21–23
sex 3–6, 28, 29, 35, 38, 80, 85
sex discrimination 80–82, 85
shrink it-pink it opinion 19–21

single rate (VAT/GST) 64–66
sin tax 43–44, 54
slave taxes 88
social mobilization 37–38
standard rate (VAT/GST) 62, 65, 66,
  68, 71, 87
suspect ground 80
symbolic value 18–19, 27

tampon 11–12, 58–60, 67, 69–71, 72;
  see also sanitary protection products
tampon tax 11–13, 58–72, 75–79, 80,
  82, 83–84, 84, 86–87, 88
tax 12–13, 41–43, 52–53, 72, 75–76, 78
tax on knowledge 76, 88

use value 18, 27

VAT 43, 45–46, 59, 60, 61, 62–66, 69,
  70–72, 77, 78–79, 83, 86–87

weaker sex 21
window tax 76, 77–78, 88
woman tax (women tax) 10–13

zero rate (VAT/GST) 59, 60, 62–66,
  69, 77, 83, 86, 87

For Product Safety Concerns and Information please contact our
EU representative GPSR@taylorandfrancis.com Taylor & Francis
Verlag GmbH, Kaufingerstraße 24, 80331 München, Germany